Aspen

Music Festival

the First Fifty Years

Aspen Music Festival

the First Fifty Years

BRUCE BERGER

TIGER BARK PRESS

ISBN-13 978-0-9860445-4-0

Cover design by Debra B. Topping

Cover photo of Arthur Rubinstein by Ferenc Berko/Photographers Aspen

Tiger Bark Press
Steven Huff, Publisher
202 Mildorf Street
Rochester, NY 14609

www.tigerbarkpress.com

Contents

Acknowledgments

GRATITUDE IS EXPRESSED to the following individuals, whose generosity with their time and their memories made this account possible: Adele Addison, Debra Ayers, Deborah Barnekow, Fritz Benedict, Ilan Chabay, Marion Chabay, James Conlon, Carole Cowan, Dorothy DeLay, Cipa Dichter, Misha Dichter, Cloyd Duff, Jane Erb, Rudolph Firkušný, Elsa Fischer, Gideon Gartner, Herta Glaz, Larry Gottlieb, Judy Hancock, Gordon Hardy, Lynn Harrell, Robert Harth, Nancy Hill, Anthony Hume, James Hume, Lee Ingram, Jeanne Jaffee, Charles Jones, Bert Lewis, Cho Liang Lin, Timothy Marquand, Gairt Mauerhoff, Jacqueline Melnick, Jorge Mester, Madeleine Milhaud, Forrestt Miller, Zara Nelsova, Mary Norris, Kurt Oppens, Elizabeth Paepcke, Bo Persiko, Stuart Sankey, Nadja Salerno-Sonnenberg, Bob Schoppert, Eudice Shapiro, George Shirley, Brooks Smith, Nancy Smith, Marge Stein, Leopold Teraspulsky, Nancy Thomas, Viviane Thomas, Eleisa Trampler, Tony Trampler, Martin Verdrager, Philip West, and Yi Wu.

Thanks also to the staff of the Aspen Music Festival and School, especially Christine Nolen and Laura Smith; and to Debra Ayers, whose tireless fact-checking proved invaluable. Also, apologies to anyone who contributed their time who may inadvertently have been left off this list.

And last, thanks to the musicians and music-lovers, too numerous to name here, whose dedication over the past fifty years has made the festival and school what it is today.

Introduction

REPUBLICATION OF THESE PAGES returns to the public the half-century backstory of one of America's premier music festivals. In your hands is that story's third incarnation, which amplifies a second incarnation that had expanded the first. The original version, published by the Aspen Music Festival itself on the occasion of its fiftieth anniversary in 1999, was called *A Tent in the Meadow*, and the reader is referred to the Afterword for an account of its colorful twelve-year assembly. In the large format with advertising that is generally called a "hotel book," the first version was fine for the event but less appropriate for a permanent text, and the narrative was sold to a Colorado publisher that issued it in a handsome paperback called *Music in the Mountains*. In that form it served the public admirably for a dozen years, but the Colorado publisher was bought by an out-of-state conglomerate that chose, in high corporate style, to destroy all remaining copies without informing the author.

I felt this blow less for myself than for the Festival, which had lost the only book-length account of its creation and evolution. A quest began for its return, a local commitment fell through, and meanwhile I contemplated yet another title. I hadn't been consulted about either of the previous two, which I only learned upon publication, and while I relish lyricism and wordplay, *A Tent in the Meadow* sounded to me like a book about camping, while *Music in the Mountains*, with its facile alliteration, seemed a bit stock. Furthermore, it turned out, Music in the Mountains was the name of a music festival in Durango, which was not amused that its name was conscripted for the history of a festival in Aspen, and the phrase was used by other Colorado festivals as a slogan in promotions. Why not just announce what the book was about? It is with pride that I welcome what I trust will be this story's final incarnation: *Aspen Music Festival: The First Fifty Years.*

Nearly a decade and a half have elapsed since this story's last printing, and out of countless subsequent events I will mention only one bit of synchronicity. Just as *Music in the Mountains* ended with the replacement of the canvas tent with a permanent structure designed by Aspen architect Harry Teague, who had previously designed Harris Hall, publication of this version coincides with replacement of the old Castle Creek campus with a new one, also designed by Harry Teague. Cost of the $60 million project is shared with the site's longtime non-summer occupant, Aspen Country Day School, and the first phase of the Matthew and Carolyn Bucksbaum Campus – named for longtime board members and concertgoers who donated $25 million toward the Festival's half of the cost – bestows rehearsal halls, studios and practice rooms in clean, elegant, acoustically resonant new structures. Music is an invasive that can adapt to many habitats, and I am sure it will flourish in its new quarters.

Bruce Berger
June, 2014

Music for the Whole Man

SO SYNONYMOUS have music and Aspen become that after fifty summers the Music Festival seems more a product of nature than of human design. Successive tents have swelled, subsided, breathed like living creatures. Shadows of aspens toss a spangled calligraphy onto the sides while magpies streak overhead, changing shape in the folds like birds of shifting thought. The summer festival has steeped so long in sagebrush and canvas that, as one resident put it, the music tent is as much a symbol of Aspen as the Eiffel Tower is a symbol of Paris.

Transposed into figures, the Music Festival in 1998 played to some thirty thousand concertgoers attending an average of five events apiece. Two hundred nineteen faculty members and guest artists, joined by students, gave over 260 concerts, taught 876 students, and added approximately thirty-two million dollars to town coffers. Numerous faculty members have bought homes, more return annually, and to many itinerant musicians Aspen, on two-month stopovers, is the closest approximation to home. While music in such surroundings may seem a case of spontaneous generation, the Aspen Music Festival, in fact, results from dedication and sweat, along with a timely series of accidents, follies, manipulations and blind luck.

Aspen does have a musical prehistory that dates back to the opening of the Wheeler Opera House at the height of the Silver Boom in 1889. But variety shows that included floods and fires on stage, heroines on treadmills, and Viennese fencing teams hardly qualified as opera—nor did the more modest yearly musicales staged by locals after the silver market collapsed in 1893. The idea of the Music Festival as we know it was born in the mind of a Chicago industrialist who was looking for a spot in the mountains where music could become one strand in the life of the well-rounded humanist. Unknown to him, a depopulated mining town, complete with fire-gutted opera house, was waiting to accommodate his vision.

Walter Paepcke was a kind of American Medici. Strong-willed founder of Container Corporation of America, Paepcke immersed himself in classical music, spent non-business hours with prominent intellectuals at the University of Chicago and could quote passages of Goethe's *Faust* by memory. His wife, the former Elizabeth Nitze, daughter of a comparative literature professor, shared Paepcke's view that music, combined with athletics, intellect, love of nature and integration with the other arts, could forge what their circle referred to as the Whole Man. It was Elizabeth Paepcke who first discovered Aspen, in 1939, taking houseguests on a swing through the Western Slope from a ranch the Paepckes owned outside Colorado Springs. The place struck a chord, and she led Walter Paepcke there just as World War II was about to end, in the spring of 1945. Even Elizabeth was startled that her husband was impressed enough to buy a large Victorian house in Aspen the day after they arrived.

Having found home base for the Whole Man, Paepcke moved on all fronts at once. He enlarged pioneering ski trails, cut new ones, installed chairlifts, bought real estate, formed a nonprofit corporation, cleaned up the opera house and the Hotel Jerome, and recruited as many friends as possible, by whatever means. James Hume, a Chicago lawyer who became a lifelong trustee and verbal chronicler of the Music Festival, recalled a dinner the Paepckes threw at the Chicago Racquet Club. It turned into a recruiting party. "Walter announced that he was going to open up this little town called Aspen, Colorado, a place where people could gather for intellectual discussions, scenery and music. He didn't expect to have more than a few prominent musicians at first, but maybe it would gather momentum. We were all invited." And when the Humes did spend the summer of 1947 in Aspen, they found themselves at Paepcke soirées being entertained by the concertmaster of the Chicago Symphony and harpsichordist Dorothy Layne. Even after its tidying the Wheeler Opera House was a sooty cavern with charred beams and pigeons commuting through holes in the roof, but Paepcke reopened it with folksinger Burl Ives, and filled out a program with movies from the Museum of Modern Art and an evening with tenor William Dyer Bennett. Some of the events may have played to more pigeons than people, but audiences would come later; Walter was merely tuning up.

Paepcke found his grand opportunity when Robert Maynard Hutchins, the young, ambitious president of the University of Chicago, was planning an international festival to honor the two hundredth birthday of German poet, dramatist, traveler, mathematician, critic, geologist, politician, evolutionist, global culturalist and visionary Johann Wolfgang von Goethe. Leaders of thought from around the world would be invited to celebrate Goethe's career and, in particular, to discuss how his thought applied to international postwar problems. It was Hutchins' observation that Chicago was large and distracting, and surely the festival would be much better off in the little mountain town Paepcke kept pushing, called Aspen. Aspen's very isolation would encourage focused exchange. The difficulty of getting there would ensure that participants would stay put once they arrived. The natural world, so important to Goethe, would surround them. Finally, the intellectual discussions could be complemented by a music festival, reflecting Goethe's own interest in music and featuring works by Goethe's German contemporaries and successors, many of whom had provided musical settings to his poems. Paepcke, as usual, was persuasive.

The Goethe Bicentennial Convocation and Music Festival, to cite its long-forgotten full name, is generally looked back on now as a celebration of Goethe, post-Renaissance man, by intellectual superstars of the late forties. Little remembered, by contrast, is the political context in the wake of Germany's defeat in World War II. In James Hume's perspective, "The group at the University of Chicago recalled that following World War I the propaganda had been so anti-German that it was impossible to hear Beethoven, Mozart, Wagner, any of the Germans, until the middle of the thirties. They didn't want that to happen again. They said, 'We've put the Nazis down, put Hitler down, but we want to embrace the German people.'" The idea, then, was to rescue what the Chicago intellectuals considered the best of German culture and, using Goethe as an examplar, reintegrate it with the continuing Western tradition. To place Goethe's humanism within as broad a spectrum as possible they invited, among others, the Spanish philosopher José Ortega y Gasset; Russian-born violinist Nathan Milstein, pianist Arthur Rubinstein, and duo pianists Vitya Vronsky and Victor Babin; American novelist Thornton Wilder; Italian literature professor Giuseppe Antonio Borgese; and English poet Stephen Spender. Israeli theologian Martin Buber sent a paper to be read and Finnish architect Eero Saarinen was commissioned to design a festival tent.

In view of postwar anti-German politics, it is ironic that the touchiest situation involved an American, Dorothy Maynor. Explained Elizabeth Paepcke, "Dorothy Maynor was a wonderful soprano who was black, and we invited her on purpose. We were trying to make the Goethe Festival interracial as well as international, which at that time nobody was willing to do. Dorothy and her husband stayed with us at our house. We couldn't put them up at the Jerome because we didn't want people to insult them, and people were still doing that in 1949. Walter was an internationalist who believed in the dignity of the individual. That was the whole reason for the Goethe Festival." It was, meanwhile, Mrs. Paepcke's idea to invite the indisputable star of the Festival, German theologian, Bach scholar and doctor to the impoverished in Africa, Albert Schweitzer.

It was Schweitzer, of course, who put the Goethe Bicentennial—and Aspen itself—into the American psyche. Schweitzer's actual presence in Aspen was quite brief. Correspondence inviting him to the Festival was postmarked Chicago, and because no one informed him otherwise, he assumed that Aspen was a Chicago suburb. Surviving an unexpected thousand-mile journey by train and by car to an elevation of eight thousand feet—"too close to Heaven," as he put it, for his health—he gave lectures on successive days, one in French, one in German, both translated on the spot by Thornton Wilder. Then Schweitzer left. As expressed by Norman Cousins, covering the Goethe Bicentennial for the *Saturday Review of Literature*, Schweitzer's greatest contribution lay in "the simple pragmatic fact that he was there."

The celebration itself lasted two weeks and drew some two thousand people—more than the population of Aspen itself. Blocklong lines waited for food to be doled out at the Mesa Store building. Lectures and symposia alternated with concerts by Rubinstein, Dorothy Maynor, Metropolitan contralto Herta Glaz, baritone Mack Harrell, bass Jerome Hines, violinist Erica Morini, cellist Gregor Piatigorsky and the Minneapolis Symphony under Dimitri Mitropoulos. Each of the eight concerts was given twice to accommodate the crowd. Stuart Sankey, for many years principal bass of the Aspen Festival Orchestra, remembers driving to Aspen for the day with friends from Colorado College in Colorado Springs and hearing Milstein and Piatigorsky play the Brahms Double Concerto with the Minneapolis Symphony. Repertoire was overwhelmingly, not quite exclusively,

German. Telling for the future was that many musicians wanted to return the next summer for a longer music festival, unpropped by Goethe. They were in luck, for Paepcke told them they were all welcome back.

♪♪

The Goethe Bicentennial, in retrospect, can be seen as Aspen's artistic big bang, the generating explosion from which organized culture in Aspen separated out. So intoxicating was the fusion of deep thought, music, mountains, canvas and summer dust that no one, least of all Paepcke, was willing to dismiss it as a one-time event. Music and intellectual discussion were formalized as the Aspen Institute of Music and the Aspen Institute for Humanistic Studies, their very names reflecting their pairing as complementary halves of an evolving dialogue. Musicians attended lectures, lecturers attended concerts, and for members of the public who attended both, they were braided strands in a life of the spirit.

Mack Harrell and Herta Glaz accepted their invitations to return. Paepcke wanted a lieder singer and at Herta Glaz's suggestion invited Leslie Chabay, who sang at the Metropolitan Opera in New York but preferred the concert repertoire. The Paganini Quartet, brandishing four Stradivariuses once owned by Niccolò Paganini, played chamber music, along with the Juilliard Quartet and the Albineri Trio. The Denver Symphony Orchestra, seventy-five members strong, was well-positioned to play both as individuals and en masse, and music director of the Festival was Joseph Rosenstock, conductor of what the *Aspen Times* called the "German wing" of the Metropolitan Opera. There was even another German bicentennial to celebrate, for Bach had died in 1750, one year after the birth of Goethe.

Teutonic entertainment began, however, with a weeklong Wagnerian extravaganza featuring tenor Lauritz Melchior and soprano Helen Traubel, and opened with the Denver Symphony

Orchestra performing "The Entrance of the Gods into Valhalla" from *Das Rheingold*. Melchior and Traubel sang selections from *Die Walküre*, *Lohengrin* and *Tristan und Isolde*, and rain pounded and thunder clapped when the Denver Symphony Orchestra played the overture to *The Flying Dutchman*. There may have been some nervousness about Wagnerianism—not least because the reputation of Traubel's predecessor, Kirsten Flagstad, had been smirched by untimely performances in Nazi Germany—for Traubel's publicity stressed her own national purity. "She has studied entirely in the United States—is an all-American product ... one of the most avid baseball fans in the country, Helen Traubel is a real American." Italicizing the point, Traubel went to Maroon Lake and exclaimed, "It's breathtaking—spectacular! Nothing in the world is more beautiful—Switzerland cannot equal it. We Americans should blow our own horn more—we are too modest about the American grandeur." Melchior more quietly caught a fourteen-inch trout in Castle Creek. Of their final concert, the *Aspen Times* wrote, "the exhilarating odor of rain-soaked alfalfa in the fields surrounding the amphitheater and the darkened sky lent a mood to the afternoon performance of the fervent 'Siegfried's Rhine Journey.' ... Miss Traubel triumphantly closed the concert with Brünnhilde's 'Immolation' and was received with an appreciative ovation by a thrilled audience."

After immolation in Wagner, Bach came to the fore with no fewer than seven cantatas and performances on the harpsichord and electric organ by Fernando Valenti. The surprise star of the summer, however, was Igor Stravinsky, who conducted the Denver Symphony Orchestra in two performances of a concert that included his *Divertimento* and *Firebird*, and Tchaikovsky's Symphony No. 2. Tony Hume, young son of James Hume, sneaked into the Tent for a nighttime rehearsal. Many of the Denverites, particularly the percussion section, had been hit with "Aspenitis," epidemic diarrhoea loosened by Aspen's defective water system, and those still functional scrambled frantically to keep up with the demands of *Firebird*. One young man played the triangle with one hand and the snare drum with the other while kicking the bass drum. When the percussion section collapsed in exhaustion at the last bar, the composer had the rest of the orchestra stand up and applaud them. Stravinsky himself had to improvise when his luggage failed to show up in time for the first performance, forcing him to conduct in jeans and tennis shoes.

Aspen Institute participation began with Robert Maynard Hutchins speaking before the first concert, then presiding over a humanities program that included Mortimer Adler teaching his Great Books course with such participants as Clare Booth Luce, and guest speakers that included the minister from Lebanon lecturing on "The Ontology of Man in Plato's Republic" and Reinhold Niebuhr explaining "Augustine's Conception of Selfhood." Paepcke had set up a casual restaurant outside the Tent; Marion Chabay, wife of Leslie Chabay, remembers chatting there with editor Norman Cousins and physicists Leo Szilard and Enrico Fermi. The Institute and the Festival were brought into close conjunction when music critic Olin Downes said that everyone should be his own critic, then set the example by saying that as far as he was concerned, Stravinsky's *Divertimento*, which the composer was to conduct in a few days, was "musically void."

The season concluded with two notable events, the more prominent at the time being the last concert, a Gala Benefit Concert Program, with half the proceeds divided between the Aspen Community Church, St. Mary's Catholic Church and the Pitkin County Hospital, and the other half going to the Aspen Institute. The program was selected from ballots printed in the *Aspen Times*, and the event was an obvious gesture to involve the town and generate support for a program imposed by outsiders. More portentous for the future was the first student concert. While there was yet no official music school, thirty-four students had followed their teachers to Aspen, and their talents—and tuitions—had not gone unnoticed.

That first official summer of the Aspen Music Festival may have been its most idyllic. First-year glitches had been worked out at the Goethe Bicentennial and divisions that were later to complicate the staging of the Festival hadn't yet surfaced. Concerts were held in the nine-hundred-seat Saarinen Tent, with the white top and orange skirt characteristic of circus tents. Unlike the later pre-concert scramble, ticket holders were led to assigned seats by ushers uniformed in white blouses and orange skirts to match the tent. Prices were a dollar or a dollar fifty, depending on the event. The Lumpen sat on wooden benches while the Paepckes and their friends settled into comfortable chairs up front. Stratified seating may seem at variance with Paepcke's stress on the dignity of the individual, but it was congruent with reality. As trustee James Hume explained, "Paepcke collected money from individuals and foundations during the winter and the rest he picked up himself. The music cost in the neighborhood of $80,000 a year, and he just wrote a check for it at the end of the season."

♪♫

If 1950 was a year of trying to figure the basics, the next year saw the Festival take shape in a form still recognizable. At that point Tanglewood, in the Berkshires, was the only American music festival of consequence, and Tanglewood was basically the summer residence of the Boston Symphony. Other symphony orchestras did not perform year-round, and the best musicians from all corners of the United States could be hand-selected. Word spread quickly among musicians and many selected themselves. Stuart Sankey noticed that the catalog listed no double bassists, and showed up. Kurt Oppens, later program annotator for the Festival, learned of Aspen from a poster and applied for the post of piano tuner. Mack Harrell recruited pianist Brooks Smith.

Especially anticipated was thirty-seven-year-old Czech pianist Rudolph Firkušný, of whom the *Aspen Times* wrote, "The handsome young artist is also a champion mountain climber and asks his manager to route him through the mountain states." When the number of students who followed the performers to Aspen leapt from thirty-four to 183, Paepcke asked Harrell to form an official music school.

The arrival of students changed the entire complexion of Aspen in the summer. Applications at first came in so slowly that the registrar would actually track down Walter Paepcke to inform him when they received one. Such doubts were unfounded, for enrollment eventually boasted students "from thirty states plus Alaska, Hawaii, Canada and Norway." Units of college credit were granted through the Lamont School of Music at the University of Denver, and tuition for eight weeks was $280. The first scholarship for full tuition was given by cellist Gregor Piatigorsky. The Prince Albert—later the Independence Hotel—and the Roaring Fork Dormitory on what became the Hyman Street Mall were turned into student housing. More students stayed in private houses, at public campgrounds, in leafy hideouts on Forest Service land that erupted with tents.

All of these locations—and many more—doubled as practice rooms. The Roaring Fork played backup to violins and horns. When a woman who kept horses was confronted by a cello student who wanted to practice in one of the stalls, she replied that the stable was too cramped for a healthy backswing but he was welcome to serenade the pasture. Most citizens were tolerant of trumpet involuntaries, though one resident did object when a beginning trombonist set his folding chair at the property's edge and played *The Ride of the Valkyries* at a dirgelike tempo, off-key, over and over, all day. Faculty had their own complaints. A member of the Juilliard Quartet rented a house over Hallam Lake, and because its rooms were small the quartet practiced on the lawn. The Humes, next door, enjoyed the concerts, but finally became jaded enough that they played pingpong on their own lawn during rehearsals and had to be told that their games were "upsetting Mr. Mozart." George Gaber's percussion over a foreign car garage, midtown, gave cacophony a beat as students bowed, vocalized, blew, pounded and caterwauled from open windows until the whole downtown brayed like a Serengeti waterhole—or a symphony by Ives.

For students the challenge was where to practice; for faculty the adventure was where to live. During the first years, composer Charles Jones took a room over the hardware store and bassist Stuart Sankey rented a room at the Hotel Jerome for eighty dollars a month. Rudolph Firkušný occupied the writing studio of novelist John P. Marquand, and flutist Albert Tipton and pianist Mary Norris squeezed into a log cabin. Said Tipton, "We sat on nail kegs, cooked out every night, and hauled a grand piano in a trailer over the Divide." Cellist Claus Adam was almost camping out in his cabin with dirt floors and no running water. The Adams bathed across the street, fetched water, and brought in boards to support a piano; in that tiny space he practiced, taught and composed. Most quarters were unfit for teaching at all, and faculty gave lessons in the elementary school gymnasium, the basements of the Community and Catholic churches, the Wheeler Opera House, garages, private homes of consenting non-musicians, and such unbooked venues as parks and streamsides.

For many the grand adventure was the Tent itself. Saarinen's design was architecturally clever, for he did away with the central pole that would intrude on the sight line to the speaker's or conductor's podium by positioning four poles partway to the perimeter, leaving the central space unobstructed and creating a raised quadrangle rather than a peak at the tent's crown. Anchored by chains, the poles were held upright by tension pulling in all directions. For the two-week Goethe celebration it was an inspired creation, but the architect never imagined that it would be stored and repitched for a decade and a half of subsequent music festivals. "Through the flaps you could see horses running around before a storm," recalled Mary Norris. "The tent poles would bang on the cement during the wind and the chains would rattle. The old bearded caretaker would come out and batten the hatches—it was exciting." For Stuart Sankey it was more than exciting. "On a windy day the wooden poles would actually lift off the ground and you wondered whether the whole tent would topple." When downpours drummed and the audience was slight, concertgoers hauled chairs onstage and surrounded the musicians.

The Tent was already being blamed for spoiled performances: Virgil Thomson's *Stabat Mater* had to be repeated five weeks later because the first performance, in the words of the *Aspen Times*, "was scarcely heard because of the pounding of the rain on the tent top." And the Tent may have aggravated a concert performance of *Così fan tutte* during which narrator Dick Leach was running a fever, flutist Albert Tipton was into his second week of appendicitis pains and oboist Lois Wann was enduring the dread Aspenitis. Mary Norris recalled further perils. "In the early days it would rain so much there would be standing water on stage. Once Beveridge Webster played the piano in a huge puddle, tapping his feet and splashing the audience. Another time George Gaber was doing a piece for electrified percussion and all we could think of was the currents going through all that water. But even with the tiny dressing room with an out-of-shape mirror, the divas came out looking gorgeous."

For cellist Zara Nelsova the Tent almost required the circus acts it seemed designed for. "We had no warming-up place in the tent, and we couldn't make a sound in the shed because it carried. There was no connection between the shed and the tent, and invariably we had a storm before the afternoon concert. Sam Flor, the orchestral personnel manager, would hold up his big umbrella while I slithered across the board that was the only way in, holding my cello and hoping my gown wouldn't pick up the mud on either side, then walked on and played." Other species were less inhibited. When Eudice Shapiro was playing violin onstage, a large black dog bounded up to smell the artificial rose on the waist of her concert dress, followed by a Tent manager who scooped up the dog and carried him off. Gophers scurried into the Tent and dove under the stage to get away from entire packs of dogs, who would chase them as far as the stage and bark, bringing concerts to a halt until a violinist's son was designated dogcatcher.

Because of its small forces, and also by Paepcke's preference, the Festival was at first mainly a chamber festival with a guest orchestra. At the Goethe Bicentennial, with the exception of Mack Harrell, almost all the soloists were European emigrés, and only over the years did the performers tend toward the American born. Paepcke's concept was to keep the season select, "with only the best musicians, to do the things that aren't box office, that you can't find in cities. We shouldn't compete with the big orchestras and operas; we should stick with what we can do." His handful of world-renowned musicians offered polished performances of a choice repertoire while concertgoers spread out to make the Tent look fuller. Marge Stein, for thirty years a trustee, recalled programs that weren't exactly box office. "In 1951 and 1952 they had chamber music on Wednesdays, and sometimes there were only fifteen people in the audience. They played highly unknown, intellectual pieces. I learned a lot, though I didn't always like what I learned. I didn't like Bartók, then I really loved him."

Improvements in 1951 included a modest upgrade of the Wheeler Opera House. With Eero Saarinen in charge of structure and Bauhaus designer Herbert Bayer supervising décor, walls were patched and painted, a new plywood ceiling was installed to match the original plaster and lath, and the notion of replacing benches with chairs advanced to the planning stage. And unexpectedly, with more musicians on hand came a fresh possibility—the Festival's own improvised orchestra. It contained, said Stuart Sankey, "thirty-five or forty musicians, with faculty in the first chairs and the rest students. Joseph Rosenstock, the director, was very adaptable, and if there was no trombonist, someone simply played the part on the piano. The piano played all the harp parts." In Kurt Oppens' words, "There was no orchestra when we came in 1951. It was put together from students. There were string students, wind and brass students, timpani, with different teachers, and then someone had the idea to put them together. One cold evening in August suddenly there was an orchestra. It was improvised, a happening. I was thrilled."

♪♪

That air of improvisation of the Festival's first years is the more striking when it is remembered that music is a severe discipline and that, furthermore, the Festival came to being during the conformist postwar years, at the beginning of the Cold War. NATO, tellingly, is precisely the same age as the Aspen Music Festival. During the Festival's formative years, the United States was in the grip of McCarthyism. Robert Maynard Hutchins, the University of Chicago chancellor who planned the Goethe Bicentennial with Walter Paepcke, was a particular target of Senator Joseph McCarthy, who labeled him a subversive, parlor pink and dupe of the Communist Party. Trustee James Hume had been recruited by the FBI to defend visiting physicist Leo Szilard, who had worked on the Manhattan Project and wanted to patent some of his discoveries about atomic energy rather than turning them over to the United States government. Victims of McCarthyism permeated Aspen in the summer, but the town seemed free of the national paranoia. Marion Chabay remembers the sense of relief when her family drove from New York to Aspen; for them it was a haven from American politics.

Children sensed a more personal acceptance: having a singer for a father and a violinist for a mother was strange for Lynn Harrell's school friends in winter, but in Aspen it was perfectly normal. The most demanding artists arrived in a mood to relax. In behavior that would now be considered unprofessional, a player who messed up a passage might stop, step back or take a breath, and try it again, to cheers and applause if it came out right. Victor Babin, director of the music school from 1951 to 1954, wanted to give the Festival a more dignified appearance. It offended him that concertgoers arrived on horseback and tethered their transportation outside the Tent; he wanted men to show up in coats and ties and women to scintillate in formal dresses. But such protocol ran against the grain and he was able to impose his dress code only on his students and his wife. More typical of the Festival was the visit of Benny Goodman, who went fishing as soon as he arrived and was chagrined to catch nothing. When he finished his Mozart, instead of receiving flowers he was given a string of trout, which he hooked to his clarinet and paraded triumphantly offstage.

Informality and playfulness were also a consequence of the amount of free time available when there were fewer students and only three concerts a week. Musicians often gathered in one home or another simply to read through chamber scores or to explore unfamiliar works. Larry Gottlieb, son of cellist Victor Gottlieb and violinist Eudice Shapiro, remembers his parents and their friends pulling up four music stands at one house or another and reading quartets. It was usually around his bedtime and sometimes he would fall asleep to one movement and wake to another, or to another piece. When somebody got lost, they would all laugh or his mother would point her bow to some bit of the score and say, "*What?*" Characteristic were the so-called jam sessions the Chabays held every Sunday evening in a small Victorian house they rented in the West End—at which musicians jammed not only in the sense of gathering spontaneously to generate sounds, but also physically jamming themselves onto the floor, on windowsills and under the piano. Wanting an audience for his vocal students, Leslie Chabay invited friends, who

invited further friends, some of them nonmusician locals. Hosts
and guests brought food; musicians played what they liked. Jorge
Mester, later music director for the Festival, played viola. Cellist
Claus Adam played piano, as did *Saturday Review of Literature*
editor Norman Cousins, who accompanied Schubert songs from
memory.

The tradition has survived over the years, but tenuously in an
ever more tightly scheduled Festival. During the sixties, Lynn
Harrell and James Levine joined violinist Robert Mann to read
through scores for pleasure. Violist Nancy Thomas remarked,
"When I was first here I played after dinner with Eudice Shapiro,
Ruggiero Ricci, Claus Adam and Bobby Mann, and I would have
to be careful not to drink too much so I could hold my own."
Impromptu music-making today is more likely to revolve around
certain teachers and their students, while the after-dinner musi-
cale has become a memory of the first decades.

These years seem idyllic, full of rebellious fun, and yet seams
began to appear, between musicians themselves and, increasingly, between the musicians and Paepcke. One item of con-
tention seems an extension of the spirit of parody. A group of
musicians and local sports formed a Rodeo Club and held
rodeos in a riding ring near the Tent on Sundays, before the concerts. Paepcke became enraged, partly because he thought
rodeos lowered the tone, and partly because local businesses
kicked in twelve thousand dollars for a rodeo grounds near But-
termilk while pleading poor when it came to supporting culture.
Said Marge Stein, "Musicians had more time in those days and
were happy to go to a rodeo before performing in the tent.
Walter said he wouldn't put up with it because it was concert
day. Herta Glaz led the parade on horseback, waving the American flag. Reporters from the Denver papers got hold of the
story, played it up big and billed it as Culture vs. Manure. That's
when Walter decided he wanted to get rid of the music."

Another source of discontent was the growing Music School,

which Paepcke had asked Mack Harrell to organize once students were on the spot but which had never been part of his plans for a peerless chamber festival. He was not amused, therefore, when, as trustee Nancy Smith put it, "police were summoned to the Roaring Fork Dormitory at two in the morning when the students were having a gala with toilet paper streamers out the window. The administration tried in vain to make Little Nell off-limits because students were always climbing up the mountain and falling off. There were housemothers in charge, but it was more than they could deal with. At one point Walter wanted to give up on the school because of having to deal with the families of students who got pregnant."

Martin Verdrager, former Festival administrator, tried to fathom Paepcke's attitude. "I feel that Paepcke did a phenomenal thing in bringing these forces together, and I know he tried to hold it together, at least through 1954, as one big unit. In 1954 he wanted to destroy the musical part, wanted it just to dissolve. He couldn't see the musicians' sense of the business end, as current trustees still can't. It's hard for them to believe that people actually want to do something without making money. They think that people should be making money, and musicians will accept less, for a sense of art. So we accept less money than they think we should. Paepcke either didn't respect that, or didn't understand it. He also couldn't handle what musicians were doing to each other, the in-fighting. That does happen, especially if there's no strong leadership in the center." Elizabeth Paepcke elaborated on the latter point. "Walter had put in as director the pianist Victor Babin. The musicians resented that Walter had elevated one of their peers, no matter how good a director and musician. It caused jealousies and disruption."

The musicians as a group also had their grievances. Said pianist Brooks Smith, "The musicians weren't happy about just being hired and coming here. We decided we needed a voice in what was going on. That's when Paepcke decided he wasn't interested—he wasn't happy with the musicians wanting authority." Added composer Charles Jones, "It seemed to us Walter had the idea of a kind of Salzburg, with very big names. We represented a high level of people who didn't command the top fees of Heifetz or Horowitz. The notion seemed to be that if Walter dissolved the Festival, he would still have a Festival by invitation as the entertainment adjunct to the Institute. We wanted to stay, and we could only stay if we separated from Walter. The split from Walter was a palace revolution." For Albert Tipton, the bottom line for Paepcke was, literally, the bottom line. "Paepcke had to change the operation because there was a change in tax laws and he could no longer take it off his income tax." In a consummate irony, Paepcke offered musicians the choice of being paid in land instead of money—an option that would have made their fortunes—yet most demanded to be paid in cash, lest they be cheated by a Chicago industrialist.

The man at the center of all these conflicting emotions, either because he was caught in the middle or deliberately put himself there, was an old Chicago friend of Paepcke's named Richard Leach. While Paepcke had given Victor Babin authority to make certain musical decisions, for three years Richard Leach was charged with running both the Institute and the Music Festival, was Paepcke's cultural vicar, and kept a New York office for managing Aspen business in the winter. Despite representing Paepcke before the impending split, Leach had been a booking agent for many of the musicians and was immensely popular with them. Marion Chabay found him so outgoing that at first she didn't trust him, then decided he was genuine. "If someone from Aspen was singing in Buenos Aires," said Jones, "Dick Leach would send flowers. That wasn't exactly Walter's financial style." Tipton's assessment of Leach—"we all loved him, he was a good man"—was not shared by Elizabeth Paepcke. "Leach was the kind of character who saw the truth two ways. He would agree with Walter that expenses had to be cut because Walter was paying all the deficits out of his pockets. After all, we'd sold our ranch on the Eastern Slope to help pay for the Festival, made sacrifice after sacrifice. Dick would then go to the musicians, who would quite rightly make an outcry about having to reduce any part of it. Of course they never realized Walter's financial position, and Dick didn't tell them why the orchestra should be kept small. I blame Dick Leach for having caused the whole trouble." Sydney Hyman, in *The Aspen Idea*, without mentioning Leach by name, suggests a powerful argument he might have used with the musicians: that Paepcke wanted to rotate performers, and if they wanted to keep coming they had better see to it themselves.

Through all of these conflicting motives and explanations, some of them contradictory, one senses that it finally boiled down to power: Paepcke wanted control over the musicians; musicians wanted control over their own destiny. Into these tensions came the crucial rift, between Paepcke and Richard Leach. No one seems to know now—and perhaps didn't know then—the specific content of the quarrel, only that it was a personality clash, and that it came to a head when Paepcke announced that he was going to close the Festival's New York office, which Leach ran. James Hume believed that Paepcke intended to reopen the office once Leach was safely gone. About the intensity of feeling, Elizabeth Paepcke was quite specific: "Walter almost had a nervous breakdown over Dick Leach. He couldn't swallow and digest his food. Dick Leach was playing both sides against the middle."

The tensions finally broke at a meeting that Paepcke convened in the Hotel Jerome to announce to the musicians that he was firing Richard Leach. Memories later disagreed on the ingredients of that meeting, though all might have been true for one occasion or another, for there were many meetings in the first one's wake as participants tried to pick up the pieces. Leslie Chabay's son Ilan, too young to understand the issues, remembers a swirl of worry and concern, along with his father's going to meetings that weren't his style. Paepcke told the musicians that they were biting the hand that fed them, and he was withdrawing use of the Tent. Clarinetist Reginald Kell gave a passionate speech in Leach's defense. It came out that Paepcke had been raising money for the Institute and the music as a package, but music was the main expense.

Courtlandt Barnes, a music-loving banker who had been invited to Aspen by Vronsky and Babin, threatened to take the Music Festival to Basalt. Nate Feinsinger, one of the nation's top labor negotiators, tried to mediate, but the musicians thought their best representative would be James Hume, who was camping up Hunter Creek. They dispatched a jeep to pick him up, leaving his wife and young son to return over a road they were ill-prepared for. Hume told the musicians that they should form a nonprofit corporation under Colorado law and raise the same amount that Paepcke did. In what was surely the most dramatic moment of that stormy evening, Herbert Bayer, the Bauhaus designer Paepcke had brought to Aspen to develop the Institute buildings and renovate Victorians, told Paepcke that he had lost sight of his vision and was preaching humanism without practicing it. It was a risky move, but paid off, for Paepcke admitted that Bayer was right, relented, and shortly thereafter told the musicians they were still welcome, could use the Tent and dormitories, but that he would no longer support them financially. To an *Aspen Times* reporter Paepcke stated that he was withdrawing from the music for "reasons of health, nervous energy and available time." It was a victory for the musicians in that they still had the Festival, along with the freedom they'd asked for, along with that freedom's obligations.

The chief obligation was to raise seventeen thousand dollars to keep the Festival going. Paepcke had tried to fundraise locally and been rebuffed, partly, no doubt, because of heavy-handedness. He thought that locals with no involvement in culture should donate money and time, and tried unsuccessfully to get one of the grocery stores to cancel a large bill that had been run up by the Goethe Bicentennial. His notion that businesses should donate five percent of their gross to the music and the Institute, as Marge Stein remarked, went over about as well as his offering lifelong Aspenites free paint if they would paint their houses the color of Herbert Bayer's choice. But as the Festival gathered momentum, businessmen did start making money from concertgoers, faculty, and students, and realized they had a financial stake. Musicians pled their cause and formed what Tipton called "a conga line all over town." Some businessmen were willing to give as long as they were assured they wouldn't have to attend concerts. To the musicians' own amazement, they raised the sum in three weeks. Proof of their success is that as soon as they were solvent, Paepcke tried to mend fences and reincorporate the music with the Institute. The musicians, pleased with their independence, weren't tempted.

The next major task was to restructure the Festival. During meeting upon meeting, as Charles Jones put it, "we made bylaws, and bylaws to amend bylaws." What they came up with was a seventy-member corporation consisting of thirty-five musicians and thirty-five nonmusician trustees, serving on separate boards. Within their group the musicians elected an administrative board that had responsibility for artistic decisions and for hiring and firing musicians, and three of their members also served on the Board of Trustees. The musicians raised money in the course of their activities—performing and teaching— while the trustees were to fundraise, find housing and supervise the properties. The Festival was renamed Music Associates of Aspen, and the Music School was incorporated within the Festival. Structurally, there was no other organization in the country like it. Courtlandt Barnes was elected first chairman of the board, and Mack Harrell recruited Norman Singer, a psycholo-

gy teacher from the Juilliard School in New York, to be Festival
dean and eventually Festival manager.

While such splits and changes of direction are as often set off
by personality disputes as by divergent goals, the musicians'
"palace revolution" did shatter Paepcke's goal of braiding music
and the intellect into strands of the Whole Life. No longer were
discussions and concerts conceived as halves of a unity. The
Institute, many have felt, became hermetic, off-limits, focused
on the powerful invited to its seminars, even as the music proceeded to break attendance records, become a national event
and, in some later views, cater to box office in a way that
Paepcke would have shunned. The Institute and the Festival increasingly resembled an old married couple compatible from
separate bedrooms.

Elizabeth Paepcke was embittered enough by the break that
she didn't talk to the rebel musicians for a couple of years; then
she relented and all was well. She also added a curious postscript
to the Leach affair. "Mack Harrell and Reggie Kell, who had really spearheaded the revolt against Walter, later received all of Walter's files and his correspondence, and realized how wrong they
were about Walter being able to pick up the deficit. Two years
after the blowup, when Walter was dying of cancer in Chicago,
they came to me and admitted they had made a great mistake.
Would I please tell Walter."

Lunacy and Discipline

DETACHED FROM PAEPCKE, the Festival rapidly grew, leavened by students. In musical matters Norman Singer, new Festival administrator and dean of the music school, was severe enough to hold that Shostakovich's Symphony No. 1, though modernist, was too popular to play in Aspen. He had been impressed with the talented students at Juilliard and thought that rising talent in Aspen—often the same talent—should be featured on the programs. Students were scheduled as soloists and they filled in the orchestra. The high quality chamber programming that Paepcke thought should comprise the whole Festival was now only a component in a student-oriented organization. The most highly attended event of the week, the Sunday afternoon orchestral concert, doubled as a teaching opportunity that allowed students to rehearse with professionals, then perform with them in public. So successful was Singer at firing up his winter students to participate in the experiment—or so eager were the students to follow Norman Singer—that Aspen was sometimes referred to as Juilliard West.

Albert Tipton promoted the idea of a second orchestra composed exclusively of students, though launching it didn't prove easy. "We had to compete for equipment, and haul chairs and stands and scores back and forth from the Tent to the Brand

Building, over the garage. Then William Steinberg, who was Festival director in 1954, raided fourteen of our best players for the regular orchestra and left us short—we were so good. He and I had a big rhubarb over that." With the addition of the second orchestra, the emphasis on students increased.

The ability of students to rise to prominence became clear in the first year of Norman Singer's tenure when Carlisle Floyd, a piano pupil of Rudolph Firkušný, showed an opera he had written to soprano Phyllis Curtin, hoping to lure her to Tallahassee the following winter to sing in its world premiere. Although Curtin had never heard of Floyd, she invited him to her house, where he explained the plot and ran through two of the arias. When he offered to play more, she said it wasn't necessary, for she had already determined to take the part and, furthermore, she would show Mack Harrell the splendid role for him. When Curtin informed Firkušný that his student Carlisle Floyd was a composer, a surprised Firkušný commissioned Floyd to write a piano sonata. Firkušný performed the sonata numerous times in New York, and as for the opera, *Susannah*, it was so well received at Florida State University that the following winter it was performed by the New York City Opera and won the 1956 New York Music Critics' Circle Award. *Susannah* has become a permanent contribution to the American opera repertoire, and when it was performed by the Aspen Opera Theater Center in 1998, with the composer in attendance, Floyd told the story of how the dream cast that brought it to attention was put together in Aspen when he was a piano student, forty-four years earlier.

One student who arrived during that period, a singer invited by Mack Harrell, took it upon himself to organize all-student concerts. Forrestt Miller got teachers to recommend pupils and to take responsibility for the quality. Under Miller's care the program expanded to three programs a week—in the Tent, the Opera House, the Community Church—with special events scattered through town. Miller's signature event, begun the year he arrived, was the annual Uncle Forrestt concert for children. Held in the elementary school gym after debuting on a church lawn, his programs over the years featured such attractions as a six-year-old violinist who grew up to become Sarah Chang, the Oom-pah-pah Band from the Red Onion, and John Denver. Commented Miller, "We held the price at twenty-five cents for those from nine months to ninety years old. All others were admitted free if accompanied by both parents. That kept out the crashers." At the thirty-fifth Uncle Forrestt concert, in 1988, two women who had participated as children brought their grand-children. Said Miller of his performers: "I prefer to call them artists rather than students, because the only difference is that they lack middle-age and a great name."

♪♪♪

Growing with the Festival, less visibly than the students, was the program for contemporary composers, initiated in 1951 by French composer Darius Milhaud. There are two versions of how Milhaud first reached Aspen. Charles Jones, who was teaching composition in Santa Barbara with Milhaud in 1950, says the director of the music department of the Music Academy of the West wanted to move, called on Walter Paepcke in Chicago, and sold him the Santa Barbara composition faculty "like a baseball team." In a more genial version, Igor Stravinsky ran into Milhaud in Santa Barbara and said, "I just came from this beautiful place in the mountains. Why don't you get involved in it?" Encouraged or not by Stravinsky, Milhaud did get involved. In August the prolific Milhaud attended the world premiere of his eighteenth quartet, completing a goal he had set thirty-nine years earlier to write eighteen quartets during his lifetime—one more than Beethoven. For the composer that consummation was also a beginning, for he found that among Aspen's seductions was a dry climate that alleviated his arthritis. He established the Conference on Contemporary Music and stayed sixteen summers. Even

Aspenites with no interest in the Festival were aware of the presence in the wheelchair, for the man's size and immobility—the wide, aging round head with its black, slicked-back hair—suggested something of the Buddha. His wife Madeleine taught French diction in 1951 and went on to teach opera production in the French manner and to stage numerous operas—some from the standard repertoire and some by her husband, who had to be carried by students up the fifty-four steps of the Opera House to attend productions of his own works.

Despite Milhaud's prominence as a French composer, the man who came with him from Santa Barbara to become co-director of the composition program was an American, as were most of the composers invited at first, including Aaron Copland, Elliott Carter, Jacob Druckman, Walter Piston and Virgil Thomson. Arriving slightly later were such prominent Europeans as Olivier Messiaen and Iannis Xenakis. Benjamin Britten was invited by the Aspen Institute rather than the Music Festival, being the first recipient of its Aspen Award. Peter Schickele and Phillip Glass, who gained popular followings by very different routes, were students the same year. David Del Tredici switched to composition class when he didn't like his piano teacher. Such conversions followed a pattern Jones saw in composition students. "Sometimes players turn to composition after they've been virtuosos. Composition isn't muscular, you don't have to start at age five, so composition students tend to be older than players. And because they don't have to be prodigies, you don't have to push them."

Though the Festival branched and consolidated during the post-Paepcke era, it retained its intimacy. Faculty and students went to all concerts, and frequently players knew everyone in the audience as well as everyone onstage. Aspen was inexpensive enough that musicians brought their families and treated it as a working vacation. Nancy Hill, who first arrived as a student in 1957 and became principal second violin of the Aspen Festival Orchestra, remembered the financial casualness. "I was very proud the year that I broke even. If the artists and teachers stayed home in New York and carried on with their usual life, I'm sure they'd make more money." Musical and social lives overlapped, binding participants to each other and to the Festival. All musicians had a pass to the Hotel Jerome pool, a crossroads where the children of musicians played while parents socialized.

For students the Festival was half parental, half patched together. Students were expected to attend all concerts and live in housing provided by the Festival, subject to periodic inspection unless other arrangements, such as boarding in private homes or camping out, had been approved. They were requested to bring their own sheets, towels and music stands. Those involved in opera productions made their own scenery and costumes. The student orchestra practised in the Armory, now known as City Hall, and classes were held in the Middle School. Rehearsals on the second floor of the Brand Building proceeded with the windows wide open. Once when they played Mendelssohn's *Wedding March*, passers-by on Galena Street paired off and walked in procession. Courtlandt Barnes, president of the Board of Trustees, turned pages for pianists. If Norman Singer was strict musically, he was otherwise a free spirit. He declared Monday a compulsory day off. No concerts, lessons or rehearsals were scheduled, and students were discouraged even from practicing. Recommended activities included hiking, fishing, riding the chairlift—anything but music. The highlight of the day was a picnic for the entire Festival, faculty and students, at Maroon Lake, at the Grottos, at someone's ranch, at one of the public campgrounds. During Singer's tenure the Festival sometimes stretched to a tenth week in September, and one Labor Day it snowed on the Saarinen Tent. Musicians threw snowballs during rehearsals, and as the snow thickened, arrows were shot upward from inside, creating small punctures so the canvas could drain. The snow continued, the Tent was declared to be dangerous, and the concert was moved to the Opera House.

At that point the power failed. There was no thought of canceling, and the performance continued by lantern and candlelight. Said Brooks Smith, "I remember playing a trio, and they put a candle on either side of the piano on little tables." Said cellist Zara Nelsova, "People came covered with blankets and the performers wore huge sweaters. I didn't, because the minute I pick up my cello I'm warm. I never feel cold unless I'm away from my cello." Said singer Adele Addison, "Because there was no heat we all wore long underwear, even Zara." Said bursar Elsa Fischer, "As an encore, Adele sang 'Shall We Gather by the River.' It was a magic evening."

It is hard, from the standpoint of today's hyper-scheduled Festival, to realize how much sheer leniency, even lunacy, was permitted during the early years. Norman Singer, a purist about classical programming, called square dances in the street between the grocery and the hardware store, and sometimes attended Monday picnics in a red-lined cape, accompanied by soprano Jennie Tourel in tight jeans and high heels. When Tourel wolfed eight trout at a feast prepared for her by the Chabays, they invited her to go fishing. She showed up wearing sequined toreador pants and platform shoes and when asked, later, what she caught, she replied, "Gefilte fish."

The Festival maintained a lively sense of humor about itself. At a fundraising ball at the Hotel Jerome, Roman Totenberg and Walter Trampler played with one violin and one cigarette, passing the violin, the bow and the cigarette so as to keep the music going and the tobacco burning. In one of the odder themed events, for $1.25 you could eat a trout dinner at the Red Onion while listening to Schubert's *Trout Quintet*. At end-of-season parties at the Roaring Fork Dormitory, the faculty entertained the students. Leslie Chabay gave voice lessons as Professor Malavoce; Stuart Sankey narrated a history of the "viol bass"; Adele Addison sang show tunes; and Edith Oppens gave piano lessons to composer Charles Jones, who played the child prodigy in a Lord Fauntleroy costume.

Open to all concertgoers were nights of musical parody at the Opera House, some organized by a student named Peter Schickele who has since made a career of presenting works by a composer he invented in Aspen, the infamous P.D.Q. Bach. Programs were filled with mock lessons and excruciating recital pieces, including selections from "101 Twelve-Tone Melodies for the Solo Violin the Whole World Loves." Victor Gottlieb, dressed up as the rich, ear-wrenching diva Florence Foster Jenkins, lip-synched her recordings, contorting his face on the high notes, while Eudice Shapiro in a tuxedo pretended to accompany on piano. On one occasion Schickele made a tardy stage entrance swinging from a climbing rope, explaining he had been detained on the Maroon Bells.

Students were by no means the youngest group associated with the Festival, for many of the faculty had young children who returned every summer and did much of their growing up in Aspen. With such parents as Mack Harrell, Leslie Chabay, violist Walter Trampler, violinist Roman Totenberg, cellist Victor Gottlieb, tuner and annotator Kurt Oppens, piano teacher Edith Oppens, flutist Albert Tipton, clarinetist Reginald Kell and percussionist George Gaber, they were known collectively as Festival brats, and their behavior became legendary. The Harrell brothers climbed the Tent to its apex during concerts. While Medill Barnes was perched over the Wheeler Opera House stage working the lights for a performance of Stravinsky's *L'histoire du soldat,* he and Tony Hume aimed wads of gum at the bald pate of conductor William Steinberg. All of them mimicked the accents of the mostly foreign musicians. "Do not look at ze piano like zat, eet ees paid for," they would shriek with a tossing of hands. Some of the American offspring had lost so much credibility about pronunciation that they weren't trusted to do a favor. Ilan Chabay overheard his Hungarian father rehearsing for the American premiere of Britten's *Serenade for Tenor, Horn and Strings* and singing "Blow, buggle, blow!" Ilan popped in and said, "It's *bugle,* Dad, not buggle," but having recently told his father that the plural of moose was meese, he wasn't believed and other authorities had to adjudicate. Ilan Chabay also remembers the Harrell brothers pushing him into the deep end of the Jerome pool with his clothes on. Young Chabay and the young Harrells slid down the mine dumps behind the Boomerang Lodge, fun that sometimes degenerated into bloodletting rockfights. So terrifying was the Harrell family that they were never allowed to rent the same house twice.

There was, to be sure, a certain tension between young high spirits and music-making, as when Ursula Oppens left games with her friends in tears when her mother, piano teacher Edith Oppens, screamed for her to practice. As far as Nina Totenberg was concerned, the chief merit to concerts was that they subtracted adults, creating a market for babysitters. Larry Gottlieb, on the other hand, had a pass to the Festival and gladly attended all concerts, sometimes with score in hand; though he couldn't read music, he could count the measures and enjoyed following the ebbs and swells.

Most Festival brats didn't become musicians; they became picture framers and computer programmers. Ilan Chabay designed science museums, Larry Gottlieb became mayor of Basalt and Nina Totenberg became a prominent commentator for National Public Radio. But some did follow their parents into music. Ursula Oppens survived her compulsory practicing to become a leading interpreter of the contemporary piano repertoire. Viviane Thomas, daughter of a literature professor and a painter, hung out with the children of musicians and became a soprano.

Tony Hume remembered Lynn Harrell as "a little muscular kid with a buzz cut" and says, "I was astounded when I learned that Lynn the cellist was the same person I knew as Lynn the terror." Marion Chabay says that "Lynn was devilish until he got the cello," and the first concert Harrell himself can remember attending, between the ages of ten and twelve, can stand not just for a seminal moment in his own life, but also for the kind of consuming event that marked the first seasons of the Festival.

"My father sang Schubert's *Winterreise* with the pianist Leonard Shure. It takes up a whole evening and that was the only time it was done complete in Aspen until recently. It was the first time I was so deeply moved and had so many conflicting feelings. I wanted to cry, to shudder with fear, and I also sensed the energy of everyone being entirely rapt in what was going on, which was a singer and a pianist at the height of their powers, delving, working deeply, bringing Schubert's music alive. I never knew that music could be so powerful and communicative. There was no intermission and I felt a great pride when the concert ended. There was a long silence, then people were laughing and crying. It was a cataclysmic emotional experience."

♪♪

The years when Norman Singer was Festival administrator and dean of the Music School were marked by the invention of the post-Paepcke Festival, musically disciplined, extra-musically free-wheeling. The transition to growth and consolidation under a less flamboyant personality was unforeseen. In 1962 Singer wanted an assistant dean for the School, ran into Stuart Sankey at a recital by Aspen pianist Beveridge Webster at Town Hall in New York, and asked if he had any suggestion. At that moment a Juilliard faculty member, Gordon Hardy, walked by, and Sankey said, "What about him?" A professor of music and litera-ture, Hardy had degrees in piano, composition and had coau-thored a text on harmony, rhythm, structure and the materials of music that was used in over a hundred colleges and universities. Norman Singer hired him, then unexpectedly resigned a week after Hardy's arrival. Barely unpacked, Hardy was promoted to full dean. Singer's job was split in two and James M. Cain, brought in by Walter Susskind, became director of the Festival. Hardy assumed that post as well in 1977, holding both positions until he resigned from the Festival, twenty-eight years after his arrival, in 1990.

Throughout his tenure Hardy acted on the principle that the students were at the core and that the rest of the Festival unfolded from the School. Even though he was a Juilliard professor and became dean of its school as well, he was sensitive to the charge that Aspen under Singer was accused of being "Juilliard West." He actively recruited students from schools around the country and threw himself tirelessly into fundraising, auditions, the quest for scholarships, the production of brochures—anything to further instruction. He favored faculty members who could teach as well as perform, and persuaded non-teaching artists to hold master classes. During his first years he performed such mundane tasks as dormitory bed checks and hot dog dispensing at Monday picnics. He focused on the individual as well as the aggregate. He persuaded the eighteen-year-old inexperienced James Conlon to audition for Juilliard, which led to summers in Aspen, then a successful conducting career; Conlon credits Hardy's early and seemingly unwarranted faith as a crucial link in his career. When Deborah Barnekow, eventually the Festival's first fulltime education director, was an impoverished vegetarian oboe student living in a tent, Hardy brought her fresh vegetables. Every year at their house the Hardys held a well-provisioned lunch or dinner so that faculty members could get to know each other. When Lillian Hardy presented her husband with an ultimatum in 1977—give up being dean of Juilliard or of Aspen—he gave up Juilliard.

As Hardy busied himself with the School, the Festival's physical resources were upgraded on several fronts. Most conspicuous to the public was the replacement of the Saarinen Tent with a larger one by Herbert Bayer, in 1965. The replacement of one tent with another would seem mere upkeep, unworthy of public debate, but such is not the case in Aspen, where all changes are lurking battlegrounds for passionate, committed individuals. It was conceded that the Tent was not a miracle of acoustics, and that no tent could be. For reasons best known to meteorologists, the early years produced torrential afternoon rains far more frequently than now. Often musicians had to stop, sit it out, and start over so that their pieces could be heard, and harpsichord pieces, along with most early music, had been phased out because such fragile sounds simply did not carry. In 1960 Bayer had favored the Festival with a modest remodeling of the Wheeler Opera House, striking a compromise between his Bauhaus austerity and Victorian excess by emphasizing existing lines with black bordering, adorning the red walls with gold fleurs-de-lys. The Aspen public was therefore shocked when the Festival announced, casually in the *Aspen Times*, that what Bayer had come up with to replace the Tent was a permanent structure.

While the Tent had its detractors, it also had zealots who defended its casualness, its openness to the mountains, its very dialogue with the weather that could so frustrate musicians. Nor did the partisans of canvas all admire Bayer's buildings for the Institute, whose cinderblock geometries reminded them too graphically of the gray matter that was the Institute's focus. What most offended was the perceived arrogance of Festival officials who simply decreed a new enclosure for the music without consulting Aspenites who considered that the Festival was theirs as well. It wasn't just that Aspenites attended concerts and donated money; from the beginning they had put up music students in their houses and turned private spaces into practice rooms. They donated props, from furs to furniture, for opera productions. When the Tent was threatened by a freak end-of-summer snowfall, a local construction crew, working as volunteers, saved the canvas in the middle of the night. Angry Aspenites called for the new plans to be made public, and when the elevations hit newsprint, appearing to the uninitiated like a pair of collapsing Container Corporation boxes—rhetoric in the letters column of the *Times* accused Bayer of designing "Muzak speakers in the throes of connubial bliss." Shortly thereafter the plan was withdrawn and a redesigned tent was submitted.

The Bayer Tent increased seating capacity from 900 to 1,750 and was considered by concertgoers to be graceful and well-proportioned. The top was white, the skirt a smack-in-the-middle primary blue already known as Bayer Blue because of his use of it around town, particularly in the eyebrows over the windows of the Hotel Jerome. While the design pleased audience and architect, it did not appease some musicians. Complaints from players, who considered the Bayer Tent a step backward from the tent they had previously complained of, discharged another crescendo that crested decades later. Meanwhile, the architect was equally displeased, for musicians insisted that the chains that had secured the tent poles in place, rattling in the wind, be replaced with stabilizing cables on top, ruining the design in Bayer's eyes. Bayer had provided a triangular stage filled with cement, eliminating the hollow that had given the previous stage its resonance. When a rounded wooden platform was laid over the triangle that Bayer had drafted to be geometrically harmonious, the architect withdrew and refused to collaborate in further adaptions of the Tent. "All he cared about was design," said Stuart Sankey, an ironic stance in that it was Bayer, back in 1954, who had found the courage to remind Paepcke to practice the humanism he preached. Bayer also seemed to be reversing the Bauhaus precept, which originated with Chicago architect Louis Sullivan, that form follows function. All he cared about was form, not the tent's use. Function, meanwhile, secured an acoustical shell behind the stage, baffles adjusted for every performance, and a wooden platform elevated for resonance. Concertgoers, ignorant of this arcana, admired the new spaciousness from padded benches that replaced the penitential boards, in place since 1949.

A more significant departure was the acquisition of the Festival's first actual property, a music campus, in 1965. This self-confident move expressed a reversal from the early years when the

Festival deliberately avoided owning anything, not knowing whether it would survive and not wanting the financial liability, a wariness expressed by Courtlandt Barnes' remark, "We just want a tent we can roll up and put in our garage." By the time the Festival became a landowner, it had missed the period when building lots were selling for fifty dollars. The property itself, a mile from town up Castle Creek, had a curious history, beginning in 1879 when George E. Newman opened a mine on the spot, then converted it into a Tudor estate on the earnings. He enlarged two natural springs into ponds and modeled the main building after an English club on Piccadilly Circus, in London. In 1946 Paepcke acquired the property, repaired the buildings and opened a tennis, eating, and swimming club that served as an adjunct to the Hotel Jerome. The club was shortlived, and on Paepcke's death the property passed to Robert O. Anderson, chairman of the board of Atlantic-Richfield and president of the Aspen Institute. Anderson, in turn, conveyed the property to Music Associates of Aspen. Since the land under the Tent legally belonged to the Institute, the campus became the first property the Music Festival actually owned.

A fundraising campaign financed new teaching spaces, practice rooms and a music hall, along with a main classroom building raised as a memorial to Victor Gottlieb by his friends. A separate grant funded an opera hall. All were designed by Aspen architect Fritz Benedict, who followed the contours of the original buildings with their hipped roofs and set them by the reflecting ponds, producing an effect of Oriental calm. Construction of the practice rooms on either side of Castle Creek took advantage of red sandstone already on the spot, and the stream provided background noise, gray sound the students could amplify by opening windows. To extend Goethe's comment that architecture is frozen music, the Music School campus is an architectural harmonics in which buildings that reflect each other are in turn reflected by still water. The town may have lost its role as a raucous practice room and the students gained a small commute, but the School now possessed a haven for its proliferating activities.

In 1968 Hardy secured the Festival's first major grant, which bankrolled creation of the Aspen Chamber Symphony. The Sunday Festival Orchestra had massed forces for the big nineteenth-century Romantic pieces that form much of the popular repertoire, but the Chamber Orchestra, averaging thirty-five to forty-five players, was more appropriate for the Baroque period, for Haydn and Mozart, for concerto accompaniment and for many contemporary works. In the smaller orchestra, individuals were heard more distinctly and had to be of high quality; Festival policy, with occasional exceptions, held the maximum age of the players to thirty. The Chamber Symphony thus became a showcase for young talent, enabling students to learn a different repertoire as they shone, and the Friday scheduling initiated the now classic Festival weekend: Friday night's elegant Chamber Orchestra program, Saturday afternoon's intimate chamber concert, and the big Sunday afternoon orchestral blow-out.

A further event that set the direction of the Festival was the appointment of a long-term music director. None of the previous seven directors had served longer than six years, but Jorge Mester held the post from 1970 to 1990. He first arrived in 1955 as a chamber student with the Juilliard Quartet, and played second violin, fourth chair, with the Festival Orchestra. He returned in 1959 as a violist with the orchestra, had his own quartet, conducted Peter Schickele's first P.D.Q. Bach concert and was still pursuing his major in chamber music. In the interim, Mester had been studying conducting at Juilliard with Jean Morel. When Hardy created the Chamber Orchestra in 1968, Mester became its principal conductor, continuing in that position the following year. He had thus moved up through the ranks and as director he knew the Festival from the inside.

The nine-week summer season was only the more visible part of Mester's job, for he worked at it all year. In January and February he embarked on an audition tour throughout the United States, listening to the eight or nine hundred students who applied for instrumental and vocal fellowships, a practice he continued for fifteen years. During the same period he was permanent conductor of The Louisville Orchestra and guest conducted worldwide. In Aspen he had a reputation among musicians for being meticulously prepared for rehearsals—for having studied, pored over and mastered scores by the time he expected others to begin their first readings of them—and appeared to accomplish it all without skipping sleep. With Mester at the podium of the new Tent, Hardy at the helm of the Festival and students settled into the Castle Creek campus, the Festival passed through its burst of new growth and entered a period of consolidation at the end of its second decade: just the point that would be, for a human being, the age of majority.

Festival of Students

INTO THIS EXPANDED and stabilized setting, hundreds of new students poured. Creation of the Aspen Chamber Symphony had generated a demand for more violinists and in 1971 Jorge Mester called Juilliard violin teacher Dorothy DeLay and asked her to join the faculty. "Oh sweetie," she replied, "I thought you'd never ask." DeLay was at that time assistant to Ivan Galamian, a Russian with a strict disciplinarian style, while her own approach was the opposite, nourishing and experimental. For years tensions had been growing between them, and by accepting Mester's offer DeLay put herself in competition with Galamian's own summer music camp. DeLay thought most students would remain with Galamian and that, furthermore, they would be deterred by the airfare to Aspen. Galamian reacted by demanding that students they had taught in common choose between them, and to his shock most chose DeLay. They both continued to teach at Juilliard and even served on faculty committees together, but Galamian never spoke to DeLay again.

DeLay's Aspen career began modestly enough. Though her ex-student Stephen Clapp was on prominent display as concertmaster of the Chamber Symphony, pianist John Perry brought more students to Aspen during his first summer than DeLay. But the fifteen pupils of the first summer multiplied until DeLay's operation included a half dozen assistants, several piano accompanists and up to 150 students. 'Against the odds," she laughed, "fools poured in." Operating out of the basement of St. Mary's Church, she taught from one in the afternoon until eight or nine at night. Each of her students got time with her, though by necessity the majority of the students get most of their instruction, particularly on the basics of playing, from her staff.

As a teacher DeLay became legendary, turning out or coaching such performers as Itzhak Perlman, Schlomo Mintz, Cho-Liang Lin, Joseph Swensen, Robert McDuffie, Nadja Salerno-Sonnenberg, Nigel Kennedy, Mark Peskanov, Midori, Gil Shaham, Sarah Chang—a record possibly unmatched in the history of the violin. Other festivals trained students for the orchestra, she said, while in her opinion the young, even if they did wind up in an orchestra, needed to develop as individuals and should be trained as soloists. Her contingent, the largest cohesive block of the student body, was really a school within a school, and the way she moved it seasonally between New York and Aspen was reminiscent of the way Frank Lloyd Wright moved his architectural school, the Taliesin Fellowship, back and forth between Spring Green, Wisconsin, and Scottsdale, Arizona. Some students, such as Midori, studied first with DeLay in Aspen, then followed her to Juilliard. Just as the Festival was once called "Juilliard West," so has it been referred to as a violin festival in the wake of DeLay, and students of other instruments had to be augmented proportionally to balance the infusion of violinists. In 1970, the year before DeLay's arrival, the School had five hundred students; in 1975 it had 750.

Declared Hardy, "I want the students to *perform*—to do chamber, solo work, orchestra, to be involved with the Festival as a whole." The campus provided new venues for student activity. DeLay held recitals there twice a week, enabling students to hear classmates they only caught glimpses of during the school year. The Aspen Festival Orchestra and the Aspen Chamber

Symphony were joined by the Aspen Concert Orchestra, a student orchestra 110-players strong, equipped to perform the big Romantic and contemporary pieces, which in recent years has alternated on Wednesday nights with the Sinfonia, a smaller student orchestra that also plays for the summer's opera productions in the Wheeler Opera House. There were yet two further orchestras: the Young Artists Orchestra, which began as the DeLay orchestra to accompany violin students during Tuesday afternoon concerts, then evolved into a general concerto orchestra for strings, piano, wind and brass; and a conducting orchestra, which didn't perform in public but played on Saturday morning for a master class in which an established conductor, guiding three conducting students per class, dismembered and reconstructed a single piece until it emerged in three different versions that remained faithful to the score.

Hardy's enthusiasm and the expanded facilities prompted the Festival's single greatest burst of new programs. As if they were all turned loose at once, John Nelson founded the Choral Institute, Ted Piltzecker started the Jazz Ensemble, Claus Adam initiated the Aspen Center for Advanced Quartet Studies, Martin Verdrager developed an extensive ear training program, and Mike Czajkowski built an electronic music studio with equipment donated by the manufacturers. A guitar program, initiated by Oscar Ghiglia and continued by Sharon Isbin, each season trained roughly a dozen students who accompanied vocal students as well as performing as soloists. The Opera Theater Center and the Audio Recording Institute were launched during this outburst, and existing programs were strengthened when Paul Vermel and Murry Sidlin expanded the conducting program and Richard Dufallo consolidated on the Conference on Contemporary Music.

Remarked Albert Tipton, "Gradually we turned from being a festival of artists to a festival of students," and that student explosion at a Festival that lacked its own housing became a

logistical nightmare. A Festival employee worked fulltime on lin-
ing up lodges, dormitories, private homes, whatever could be
patched together. One of Walter Paepcke's first objections to a
school had been the supervision problems, including the potential retaliation of parents when their prodigies ran amok, and
though American culture accorded its youth greater liberties
every year, the Festival felt that its young charges should be pro-
tected as well as instructed. Dorothy DeLay's students tended to
be the youngest, and she did her best. "I initiated a dorm for children between the ages of twelve and consent on the first floor
of the Continental. It had a ten o'clock curfew and a supervisor
to cover the entrance, but I didn't realize the rooms had sliding
glass doors in back that let them right back out. I was embarrassed and apologized to one mother, promising her that I'd put
the dorm on the second floor next year. The mother replied,
'Don't bother. My daughter will only break her leg.'"

By necessity as well, students were moving out into the larger
if still sheltered world that was Aspen. Many needed funds to
make ends meet, and took jobs as waiters and waitresses, bus-
boys, check-out clerks and hamburger flippers around town.
George Shirley was startled to glimpse one of his students hack-
ing meat in the back room of City Market. Many odd-jobbing
students were publicly unrecognizable as musicians, but others
hauled their instruments to the mall and the restaurants, laid an
open instrument case at their feet for tips, and played for who-
ever would stop and listen. Solo violinists, woodwind trios,
brass quintets and all other imaginable combinations played for
passers-by, their sounds competing and overlapping, bringing
back some of the glorious musical chaos that downtown Aspen
lost when the music campus drew the students to official practice rooms.

Many restaurants hired string quartets to play inside or just
outside the door in exchange for meals and access to well-tipping
customers. Restaurant-playing became a subculture with its own

hierarchy, remembered by Nadja Salerno-Sonnenberg as a step up from working at the student cafeteria in the basement of the Wheeler Opera House. "When I was fourteen I had a busboy job to take the food off the walls when the kids left. They threw the spaghetti and powdered eggs that they hated and I made two or three dollars an hour scraping it off, thinking nobody deserves this, so I started playing in restaurants. I played in the mall, then at Guido's Swiss Inn for several summers, getting ten dollars from the restaurant, plus dinner, plus whatever landed in the tip bucket. So that was one excellent meal a day plus spending money. I also played the Souper, which had wonderful stews. Then came the great thrill. A friend of mine had *the* job of the summer, a quartet gig at the Golden Horn, then got sick and asked me to replace him. I found a replacement for myself at Guido's and thought, oh my gosh, the Golden Horn, incredible! I was thrilled."

The remoteness of Aspen, its sense of protectedness, freed teachers to experiment, and they didn't hesitate to create groups of student instrumentalists as unusual as anything the students themselves concocted on the mall. Madeleine Milhaud, diction and opera performance teacher, mounted pot-pourri programs of up to three one-act operas in different styles from Mozart to the Romantics to such contemporaries as Stravinsky, Hindemith and her husband Darius. Her coaching methods anticipated techniques later used by encounter groups and psychodrama, for she deliberately cast students in roles that contradicted their personalities: a quick-gestured person as a sluggard, a shrinking violet as a hussy. One astonished father reported that his slovenly daughter was suddenly patronizing the hairdresser and going out on dates, having found a personality she preferred. Milhaud also had students write imaginary letters while others guessed the recipients. When one student wrote her feelings to her mother, Milhaud snapped, "You're not very nice to her," then instantly regretted it. She was terrified when the student knocked on her door an hour later, but the student said, "You're right and I'm going to change things right now." In retrospect Madeleine Milhaud found her teaching methods risky, particularly considering that she knew nothing of the students' backgrounds and potential psychological problems, and later she felt lucky not to have provoked a calamity or a lawsuit.

Zara Nelsova was sensitive to the kind of student bewilderment that cropped up in Milhaud's coaching classes and developed her own way of dealing with it. "Aspen is not for every student. When the school grew, some of the students became lost here, particularly if they were the kind who didn't find it easy to make friends, and there was a kind of anonymity we didn't experience with a smaller student body. Some got terribly lonely and felt left out. I brought my students together as much as possible, held parties and kept in touch between their weekly lessons. Once when things got rough, I took them to a James Bond movie with a character who was a cellist. The position of the hand on the fingerboard was just the opposite of what I'd taught them, the cello gets damaged in a shoot-out, and in the last scene the girl plays the concerto with a bullet hole in her Strad. The whole phony scene was too much for them and a couple of them were completely hysterical with laughter, which was just what they needed."

Faculty like DeLay, Milhaud and Nelsova cared deeply for their students' welfare and their strategems were often successful in easing anxieties. Some situations, inevitably, were beyond them, and along with dorm supervisors the Festival maintained an assistance program of counselors contracted to handle more serious emotional problems. Bo Persiko, a clinical social worker employed by Aspen Counseling Center, gained insight into student conflicts during fifteen summers with the Festival.

The students counseled by him, immersed in the changes of adolescence, the tortures of growing up, had often spent their previous years studying and practicing instead of socializing with their peers, their regimes often enforced by ambitious mothers as well as mere teachers. Lacking normal social skills, they misread casual joking and banter, obsessed over glances from fellow players that referred to the music rather than themselves, coped with crushes and fretted over remarks others wouldn't take seriously. Students often watched over each other, reporting to counselors when roommates lashed out, locked themselves in the bathroom, screamed and yelled, acted drunken and despondent or appeared suicidal, and dorm supervisors were on call to field emergencies.

Interactions with adults generated further stress. Some students were terrified of conductors, particularly those who were brusk in their corrections, taking personally what was for the conductor a mere adjustment of the music. More fearsome still were the mothers, some of whom wished to live through their offspring careers they missed, others merely ambitious for a prodigy who was not always as gifted as they imagined and who suffered from the pressure. Ostensibly in Aspen to ensure their child's welfare, they lobbied faculty to get them performances in concerts and master classes, often embarrassing the student and annoying faculty to the point that Dorothy DeLay maintained strict rules for when she could be accessed by parents. Some of the mothers too became recipients of Persiko's counseling, and only once in fifteen years did he counsel a father, a faculty member concerned about a problematic student daughter.

Other adults too sought Persiko's counsel, most memorably a pair of young faculty members who courted only when they converged at the Festival and who married after the male overcame his timidity during the seventh summer. The great majority, however, were students who finally worried that the intense training to which they had devoted their growing up, both stressful and rewarding, might not lead them to jobs, let alone stellar careers. The urban conservatories they attended during the rest of the year were so demanding of their time that they repressed emotional problems, and while the Aspen Music School also required

practice, ensemble rehearsal and performance schedules, its
more relaxed atmosphere allowed stifled conflicts to flood to the
fore. It is ironic that the greater openness of Aspen, which granted some students the thrill of playing in the Golden Horn or hiking into the wilds, offered others the luxury of addressing personal problems. But if the Festival provided some students an
advance in emotional integration, it was instructing them about
life as well as music.

Over the years a blurred line between students and professionals
became a Festival trademark. In concerts arranged by Forrestt
Miller, the very young performed with such stars as Leonard
Slatkin, Robert McDuffie and members of the Juilliard Quartet.
James Levine, technically a student, conducted opera in Aspen at
the age of fourteen. Students who evolved into professionals,
partly in Aspen, include conductor and choral director John Nelson, pianist André Watts, former Festival Music Director Jorge
Mester, clarinetist Joaquin Valdepeñas, horn player John Cerminaro, conductors Murry Sidlin and Leonard Slatkin, soprano
Dawn Upshaw and Jazz Director Ted Piltzecker. Former students become names on marquees, then return as faculty.

The distinction between students and professionals is blurred
still further by musicians with careers elsewhere who come to
Aspen to study. In 1963 the principal cellist with the Pittsburgh
Symphony, Jascha Silberstein, studied in Aspen with Zara Nelsova—a tradition still healthy in 1988 when members of the fulltime professional Amati Trio came to study with Dorothy DeLay.
When Lynn Harrell left Aspen as a student of fourteen, then
returned as a renowned professional at twenty-six, he found himself performing for colleagues of his parents, musicians who had
encouraged him as he was growing up, and felt that he had
returned home and was playing for family. The demarcation
between novice and pro was not so clear for Nadja Salerno-Sonnenberg, who made an early transition from student to professional even as she continued to study with Dorothy DeLay.

Unexpectedly she was asked to perform the Brahms B major Trio with Harrell and was overwhelmed. "I knew the piece backward and forward, was very prepared, but I was still a wreck, up at five for an eight A.M. rehearsal. Lynn was so generous, asking me—*me*—what we should do with a certain passage. I was so young that I wanted to ask him, don't *you* know what to do with it? Rehearsals were so much fun that within five minutes I stopped being nervous and couldn't wait for the next one. It was more proof that the greater the artist, the greater the human being. When musicians are insecure about their playing or their standing, they have all these masks, but Lynn is one of the greatest artists of our time, and look what a pleasure it is to work with him." Student or professional, it felt like family.

Students became vivid experiences for each other, memorably in the instance of James Levine, a piano student of Rosina Lhévinne who arrived in Aspen in 1957 at the age of fourteen, the first of fifteen summers at the Festival. He seemed destined for a major career even to those who encountered him in his early teens. When Lynn Harrell first met him, he was Mack Harrell's twelve-year-old accompanist. Anthony Hume remembers him as a kid who waved his arms from his seat during orchestra concerts, practically conducting from the audience. Once when Lynn Harrell and a violinist friend were practicing the Brahms Double Concerto and needed someone to read the piano reduction of the orchestral part, they invited a pianist down the hall "who turned out to be Jimmy. Not only did he sight-read it perfectly, he understood Brahms' use of two-against-three and the hemiola as compositional devices and changed all the triplets to duplets and duplets to triplets, just for fun." On another occasion when Lynn Harrell was in the audience for a Robert Mann violin master class and Levine was to turn pages, the student didn't show up and Mann suggested they read through some Mozart sonatas instead. Levine played four without missing a note, at the end of which Mann, addressing the audience, said, "Now the question is, will he get any better?"—meaning, was improvement even possible? Despite his brilliant pianism, Levine had other goals in mind and conducted his first full opera, Bizet's *Les pêcheurs de perles*, at the age of nineteen.

Levine has said that the greatest influence on his developing sensibility was his time in Aspen, experience not limited to music. He became a close friend of Stuart Mace, a naturalist who trained huskies near the ghost town of Ashcroft and who invited music students to Monday picnics. A city boy, Levine learned of the natural world through Mace and broadened his outward connections to art and mankind to embrace other species; when Mace was terminally ill in the winter of 1993, he flew to Aspen to pay Mace a farewell visit. Levine influenced as well the students who followed him. For teenage conducting student James Conlon, the twenty-five-year-old Levine's master classes in 1969 were pivotal. "It was not so much the actual content as listening to him talk, the absolute brilliance, breadth and depth of his musical mind. It wasn't about what to do with our hands, the mechanics of conducting. When we were discussing *Don Giovanni*, he would ask, 'What is Donna Anna thinking in this scene? Why is that half note the way it is?' None of us had even considered such matters. Within ten days of classes I realized there was another level possible and necessary for a conductor, and I vowed to reach it. His classes were conversations about the basic questions of music and life, and the doors he opened in 1969 had far-ranging consequences for me."

Of the tens of thousands of students who have now studied at the Aspen Music Festival, only a small percentage have been able to enjoy major careers like James Levine and James Conlon. Most have graduated anonymously, have become orchestra players or teachers, perhaps have entered other fields entirely. There is no archetypal student experience even among those who have risen to the top of their fields. Still, it is worth following the trajectory of one alumnus—he sometimes rehearses in a T-shirt that says, on the front, "MY NAME IS CHO-LIANG LIN," and on the back, "BUT YOU MAY CALL ME JIMMY"—because it touches so many elements common to all students in its cycle.

As a teenager Lin went to a boarding school in Connecticut and took pre-college violin lessons with Dorothy DeLay at Juilliard on Saturdays. He had resolved to become a professional violinist but hadn't heard even the regular Juilliard students play, let alone such idols as Itzhak Perlman or Pinchas Zukerman, who performed at inconvenient times and at prices he couldn't afford. In 1976, at age sixteen, with DeLay's encouragement, he applied to study in Aspen, and Gordon Hardy snared him a scholarship. "Everyone told me Aspen was the most beautiful place in the world, and it was, but I was a little kid and I was far more impressed by the music. At that age you can only take in so much scenery and grandeur."

When Lin arrived at his dorm and started to unpack, he heard a Paganini Caprice coming through the window and stopped to listen. It was the most astonishing violin playing he had ever heard. "It was so good that I immediately got nervous and depressed. I thought, gee, if DeLay's kids live in this dorm and play like that, what business do I have here?" Lin traced the music to its source and knocked on the door. When a fellow student opened it, Lin said, "Hi, I don't mean to bother you, but you sound so fantastic." The student broke out laughing and the music continued. "That's a recording of Perlman," he said. Lin exhaled with relief.

Lin was made concertmaster of the Philharmonia Orchestra, the third orchestra of the Festival, a first-year achievement that made him proud. He had played in the Saturday student orchestra at Juilliard, "but when you play in little kiddie orchestras you don't play pieces like *Rite of Spring* and *Also sprach Zarathustra*. It was a revelation." He met what he called the "Dorothy DeLay whiz kids" and found the dorm a wild ride, with all the violinists practicing like mad, trying to outdo each other. Students within the DeLay circle jockeyed to perform in master classes, and rather than being intimidated by the competition he found it invigorating and jumped in. DeLay's manner was reassuring even as she taught the big pieces in public. She brought guest conductors to concerto classes, and when students stretched the music too far in quest of expressiveness, conductors pointed out that other instruments would lose the beat and fall apart.

Lin was intimidated by the idea of playing in a public class with Perlman, but Perlman put students at ease by cutting up and making them laugh to the extent that students occasionally responded in kind—as a frustrated DeLay learned when she tried to shepherd the twelve-year-old Nadja Salerno-Sonnenberg through a televised master class with Perlman. "She had been wearing the same jeans all summer, unwashed," said DeLay, "and I advised her to get a new outfit. I should have gone shopping with her, because she came onto the stage in a new pair of jeans five sizes too large, so long they wrapped around her feet. She shuffled in, chewing gum. I turned my back to the camera and hissed, 'Get rid of that gum!' Nadja swallowed it, then faced the camera pointing to her gaping jaw." For Lin, playing before Perlman in public, even without TV cameras, was a sobering prospect, but Perlman joked and DeLay positioned herself so that she remained in Lin's line of vision just behind Perlman, serene and smiling. Lin blocked out the audience, concentrated on the music, and left Perlman's master classes exhilarated.

Perlman's jovial master class style wasn't shared by Zukerman. "Pinky was a holy terror. Much the brasher of the two, he came out swinging. You'd play five notes and he'd tear you apart." Lin found it generally took him several days to absorb and incorporate new information, but Zukerman wanted immediate changes. Do this, do that: it was traumatic for a sixteen-year-old. Lin got flustered and left Zukerman's master classes crestfallen, but resolved not to be intimidated. When he returned the following summer, he intended to do exactly what Zukerman wanted and leave no room for complaint. "All of a sudden Zukerman was the most fantastic teacher. My fear disappeared, Zukerman opened up, and I learned so much. Because I could reciprocate, he gave me all the information he had." DeLay talked Zukerman into staying an extra week after the Festival, and he taught three or four students a day in the Community Church. "A staff accompanist stayed on, I played everything I'd worked on with DeLay, and there was a mammoth amount of input. Pinky was nice, relaxed, joked, had a good time, and it was the most exciting week I've ever spent. A relationship based on fear turned to a camaraderie we maintain even today."

After his first summer in Aspen, Lin changed schools, put the violin before academics and worked far harder, making his single greatest leap forward as a player. "The environment in Aspen really kicked me; it opened a whole new chapter in my life." That winter he also made his solo debut, playing a concerto with the St. Louis Symphony. Returning to Aspen "feeling like a big shot," he was assigned to the back of the second violins in the Chamber Symphony. He felt indignant at the time, and Zukerman, this time as conductor, yelled at him because he wasn't an experienced orchestra player and couldn't keep up. He later realized that demotion was just the humbling he needed, giving him the experience of those he had to play with as a soloist and demonstrating that any section may have splendid musicians he shouldn't take for granted. It also taught him the rewards of orchestra playing itself, so that he now sometimes sits in for pleasure.

In 1979 Lin graduated to the artist-faculty list, and he spent the summer of 1980 in Aspen with a full fellowship, playing one concerto and participating in an experimental chamber program with Robert McDuffie and two others. "Imagine how lazy four kids between twenty and twenty-two can get, playing only two quartets through the entire summer. We hiked up Highlands, hit the discos at night, and for the first time I realized one could have fun other than music in Aspen." In subsequent summers Lin returned only two or three weeks at a time, with such artists as Misha Dichter and Ronald Leonard. "I realized I was turning into an alumnus faculty artist," a transition that included a lot of overlap between the roles of student and professional. He finally came full circle when DeLay asked him to teach master classes. "It was hard to find the right thing to say. I had to prove I was semi-intelligent and I was still cocky enough that I needed to show the students I could play the pieces better than they could." DeLay knew how far to trust her protégé and at first only sent students who played works from Lin's own repertoire. Not until 1988 did she allow students to play for Lin whatever they wished, and he finally reached the position he had enjoyed—or suffered—under Perlman, Zukerman, and DeLay herself.

So much varied experience has given Lin perspective on performing for a Festival audience, a situation that sets off conflicting emotions in most musicians. Fellow DeLay alumna Nadja Salerno-Sonnenberg, for instance, finds that Aspen's refreshing absence of regular music critics isn't enough to set her at ease, since she feels compelled to ignore them anyway to keep playing. She enjoys, on one hand, the kindness of concertgoers who watched her grow up, endured her when she was wearing braces, and still flock to her performances, but because the Tent is packed with knowledgeable students and colleagues, she tries out new pieces elsewhere. "I'm always super prepared in Aspen because it matters to me if the conductor and orchestra like it." The sentiment is echoed by Cipa Dichter: "In spite of the fun and laughter, this is a very serious place and you don't get on stage unless you are totally ready. I'm going to see my friends the next day in the supermarket and I can't face them if I haven't played well." Confesses Misha Dichter, "Even if you are prepared—you can ask anyone—nothing is scarier than getting onstage in Aspen. Your colleagues are there and you want to play well."

Lin, at first, felt full of confidence and didn't hesitate before choosing Aspen for his first performances of various concertos:

the Bruch, the Saint-Saëns. He well remembers his psychological make-up at sixteen or seventeen, the age of deconstructing elders, when he used his ears as radar for the faintest blemish and he thought, whoa! Perlman made a mistake. Later when he played facing hundreds of young violinists, saw the area in front of the stage filled with violin cases and sensed the presence of musicians like Dichter and Kalichstein and Slatkin, he realized that in one sense nowhere, not even Carnegie Hall, was as terrifying as Aspen. On the other hand, as soon as he walked out he saw the familiar figures of Gordon Hardy standing by the entrance and Dorothy DeLay seated nearby. Aspen concerts are only sporadically reviewed in print, so a bad performance stings at first, then fades—and if the piece goes well, the deconstructionist kids will scream and holler.

However the playing goes, Lin relishes the scene backstage afterward. People surge from the audience to say hello, the reception line turns into a mob, and the moments after a performance become a time to catch up with friends. If he has played badly and feels embarrassed, well-wishers help him get over it; he thinks of backstage at the Tent as a music club, protective of its members. As for Aspen itself, it was a point of reference in his life, a measure inseparable from the presence of his teacher. Dorothy DeLay alumni never stopped being her students, and every season in Aspen, usually over a meal, Lin went over his problems, doubts and priorities with his mentor. She was the most critical listener in his life, he trusted her judgment completely, and in her mere presence he considered himself in class with her.

Lin's full tour of the Festival has included one experience that hearkens back to Paepcke's goal of combining music with the intellectual life, for he participated in a seminar on humanity and statesmanship at the Aspen Institute. He joined twelve other participants at a round table, "seven or eight executives for cosmetic or construction companies or blue jean factories, plus an English teacher, a philosopher, the director of the CIA, the ambassador to Ethiopia. They don't actively seek out musicians, but if you know someone you can be discreetly asked." All had read their Plato and Tocqueville and were to apply it to current situations. He found the seminar conservative if not overtly right-wing, felt he should inject liberal or socialist ideas if only to play the devil's advocate, and worried that he wasn't qualified to do so. The only figure from the left, a labor leader, was neutralized by being moderator, and consensus was reached quickly, without vigorous discussion. But much of the experience was extra-curricular. "Imagine sitting down to *lunch* with the director of the CIA. What do I say? I wanted to talk about Jonathan Pollock, the Israeli spy, but I thought, maybe he doesn't want to talk about those things out of the office. He was so kind, knew I was a musician, and said, 'I have a niece who plays the clarinet. ...'" Lin's co-seminarians were excited that he was to play in the Tent and he recommended certain concerts to them, which they found "relaxing." Soprano Jan de Gaetani and English horn player Philip West also attended a seminar, the upshot of having met the director of the Institute at a party; that particular program was for couples and they wound up music-making for the other couples in attendance.

But the rare and chance nature of musicians' experience of the Aspen Institute, which had been born as the Music Festival's fraternal twin at the Goethe Bicentennial, indicates how far music and the intellectual life had veered from each other; long gone, at least at the official level, was the notion that the verbal and nonverbal could be braided into strands of the Whole Life. The gap had invaded Lin himself, for when he watched Margaret Thatcher give a speech in the Tent on TV, his first thought was, "Hey, that tent is reserved for musicians—what's Thatcher doing there?"

By the time Jimmy Lin had gone through his cycle from adventurous student to seasoned professional, the Festival was old enough that its participants had matured or died or given birth: had gone through the process for which music itself is sometimes taken as a nonverbal analogue. Teachers often passed from being instructors to Dutch uncles and aunts: confidants. Dorothy DeLay ultimately coached her students about life as well as the violin, and Viviane Thomas attests that she and Madeleine Milhaud—whom she always called Madame Milhaud, never Madeleine—would go out on the town and talk about *la vie.* Many players relish Aspen as a place to enrich their children's growing up, a process described by Misha Dichter: "We see the concerts through the eyes of our children as well as ourselves. They grow up knowing that the Tent is there, that there's tennis and hiking but there's also the Verdi Requiem at four. The autumn after the Verdi, the radio was on in New York and one of our kids said, 'Oh, that's the Verdi Requiem, we heard that last summer in Aspen.' It wasn't like getting dressed up to go to Carnegie Hall and hear the Cleveland; it was coming back from tennis, hearing the Verdi, then going out to dinner. The family experience is wonderful."

The role of Aspen as a focal point for lives dispersed in global performing can be poignant as well as wonderful. When Lynn Harrell returned as a soloist in his mid-twenties, having left Aspen at the age of fourteen, he went to Leslie Chabay, whom he had known as a child, and said, "My father died when I was fifteen. Could you tell me your memories of him?"

Music in
Thin Air

CONCERTGOERS LISTENING to music on padded benches—even the unacclimatized who may have panted their way from the parking lot—may not appreciate the extra effort it takes to make music at eight thousand feet. Some, like Isaac Stern, simply stopped coming because they couldn't take the altitude. When Rosina Lhévinne reached eighty, she realized there were a lot of Mozart concertos she had never played and she resolved to learn one a year to perform, among other places, in Aspen. She did live to be ninety-six, but she lost her tolerance for the altitude and Aspen missed some of her later Mozart concertos. Those dependent on breath—wind and brass players and especially singers, who are their own instruments—are obviously the most affected and must wait to acclimatize. Little vocal or solo wind music is scheduled during the first two weeks of the Festival, and for vocalists the danger is not just a bad performance; it's damage to an instrument that can't be replaced. In the slang that even singers use for body parts that make music, you have to take care of your chops. During the early years, when Highway 82 was the only paved street through town, dust hung permanently in the air, was the smell of summer in Aspen, and the singers' oxygen-poor breaths were powdered with grit. When the streets were oiled to keep down the dust, tar fumes added a new poison. Students of vocal coach Adele Addison didn't appreciate the long and quite vertical trudge to her house at the top of McSkimming Road. Tenor George Shirley prepared for the altitude by taking brisk walks before he arrived and exercising while he was in town, primarily riding a bicycle. Not wanting to compound oxygen deprivation with heat when he performed in the Tent, he always hoped for cloudy weather.

A high altitude usually implies a dry climate, which creates its own problems. Wind and brass players cope with chapped lips. Making reeds for oboes and bassoons, time-consuming at best, is still more difficult in Aspen because reeds vibrate less readily in the reduced barometric pressure and it takes longer to make one that will work—and more concentration to play it. String players face the threat that the wood of their expensive, sometimes historic instruments will dry out. Cards with a band for humidity readings are standard equipment in violin cases, and string players, as a traditional remedy, have thrown a few orange peels into their instrument cases to impregnate the wood. Nancy Thomas's viola case was once rained on in the Tent; she rested the instrument in the case during a break, and afterward the viola sounded better than it had all summer. More high-tech are tubes with sponges on the inside, called Dampits, which are soaked two or three times a day and threaded like green plastic worms through the f-holes. In Zara Nelsova's explanation, "I leave my cello with a humidifier and a gauge so that it always stays the same. Before I learned about humidifiers, the cello would be drier and drier through the season and the strings would be so close to the fingerboard there was no tension. Also, what happens up here is that we *hear* differently. The air is thinner, which makes the sound thinner, and we all work harder to produce the sound we're accustomed to at sea level. Then during the summer you get used to it. I will hear a student say, 'My cello sounds much better now,' and the cello hasn't changed at all. When I take my cello back to New York, it sounds like ten." The problem for timpanists is that dry air causes the pitch to rise, and they insert sponges and wet rags into the holes at the bottom of the kettles, then remove them as the air chills and the note sinks. Almost every musician in Aspen lives with a humidifier to keep instrument materials from wood to lung tissue from giving out.

Not every Aspen musician, however, is an enemy of drought. If Nadja Salerno-Sonnenberg has to perform outdoors, she would much rather play in Aspen than, say, Philadelphia where "if, God forbid, it rains, it's pea soup onstage, the strings go out of tune, the fingerboard turns to molasses, you can't slide, you can't shift, and the audience doesn't realize how the instrument is affected. For outdoor concerts Aspen is ideal—though it's still not as good as playing inside." And when it comes to pianos, altitude and its attendant dryness are a big advantage according to Bob Schoppert, who has been acquiring and maintaining pianos for the Festival since 1968. "The big factor is humidity, which is very low. Pianos in New York will fluctuate a quarter of a tone within a given year, but here they stay in pitch. Pianos stored in the back of the tent have reached twenty degrees below zero without damage—extreme temperature change has less effect on a piano than four days of rain. We have hundred-year-old uprights that are structurally perfect and their finish looks like it was slapped on yesterday. Aspen is heaven for pianos."

The problem at the beginning of the Festival was that few pianos had made it to heaven. At first only the Tent had good pianos, and teaching and practicing were matters of patchwork. Few artists went so far as to haul their own grand piano to Aspen, as the Tiptons did, and most made do with instruments that were already in town. Piano-owning Aspenites opened their homes to performers and students who practiced all over the West End, on Red Mountain and on McLain Flats. The Festival acquired what pianos it could afford, then traded up. In 1963 they replaced many old uprights they couldn't keep in tune, and locals who heard about it in time were able to buy perfectly preserved Chicago uprights for between twenty-five and forty dollars—instruments that Schoppert estimates would now cost twenty thousand dollars to build. By the time of Schoppert's arrival in 1968, the Festival owned forty new Baldwin uprights that remained in practice rooms all year. A few piano teachers still taught on uprights, and the duo piano team of Jeaneane Dowis and Samuel Lipman had two pianos in their two-car garage—a grand and a spinet.

Even by 1973, when the Festival owned some ninety pianos, there was only one grand piano at the music campus, and each piano teacher was allowed to choose one student for what was called "grand time"—two-hour sessions twice a week. "I told Gordon this wasn't conducive to the type of students we had," said Schoppert, "and he gave me permission to find pianos. I called Kawai for forty grands, hoping to get twenty, and they said, 'Forty you've got.' They were here a week later, built in Japan and brought in from Los Angeles because they wanted the exposure. In 1975 Baldwin brought in pianos, all we could use, and Kawai gave us what we wanted free of charge. Students from schools all over the country say the piano situation here is the best. It's because we get new instruments every year, they're tuned, voiced and regulated, and everything works." By the summer of 1995, the Festival owned seven concert grands, supplied twenty-five Steinway grands to faculty and visiting artists, and provided 130 Steinway Bostons—Steinway-designed pianos manufactured in Japan—to students.

Pianos in the Tent must be varied as well as good, a point neatly illustrated by Schoppert. "Rudolph Firkušný once asked me to meet him in the tent. He selected a piano that he knew needed work, but he knew the compromises he would have to make and asked me to leave it alone. Alicia de Larrocha came in an hour later, tried the piano, and asked how such a terrible instrument could make it to Aspen. Alicia wanted something light and bright for Ravel and Firkušný was a hard, heavy player

who wanted a big dark sound for some Beethoven. They could-
n't stand each other's instruments but both were happy."

Schoppert has compared the arrival, placement and preparation of each year's crop of pianos to the building of the pyramids.
He shows up a month before each Festival to receive pianos that
arrive brand new in their crates from the factory, weighing
between six hundred and a thousand pounds each. It takes only
two skilled movers to place a grand, but Schoppert uses four tech
crew members to avoid mishaps. Once the pianos are lodged
where they will spend the summer, they are tuned and regulated.
During the first years of the Festival, pianos were maintained by
the Festival's first tuner, Kurt Oppens, with occasional help from
a tuner in Denver. When Schoppert arrived in 1968, he tuned one
or two pianos a day, then went fishing. By the end of the 1990s it
took six fulltime tuners and three part timers to keep 162 pianos
up to standard. Tuners pinball between the Tent, the Opera
House, the churches and schools, faculty housing, local residences
and the ninety pianos at the campus. The latter, which go out of
tune faster because of the dampness by Castle Creek, get tuned
five times a summer, and faculty pianos are tuned twice a week.
Concert pianos in the Tent receive up to ten public performances a week, and Schoppert spends roughly five weekly hours apiece
on five of them. A piano may not require much adjusting after a
performance, but every time a piano is played in public, for master classes as well as for concerts, it is retuned, and the next player gets to sample it and voice objections before performing.
Though piano students have held steady at around 150 since
Schoppert arrived, the number of pianos has exploded until there
are roughly thirty tunings a day, some two thousand over the
course of a summer. In the thick of overlapping demands,
Schoppert himself has been known to tune in the tent at three in
the morning.

In addition to between-concert tuning, Schoppert tries to be
on hand for each performance, making himself visible to the

pianist beforehand as assurance of help in case a string goes out of tune or snaps. Occasionally the problem is more exotic. Once George Shearing was to play a benefit concert on a Bösendorfer that had been used earlier in the day as a "prepared piano," which is to say that it had been rigged with nuts and bolts on the strings for an experimental piece by John Cage. Schoppert thought that he had gotten all the hardware out of the instrument, but the first time Shearing used the soft pedal to mute the tone, a stray bolt from the Cage piece fell into the pedal action and wouldn't allow the keyboard to shift back to its normal position. Shearing was forced to play the entire first half of the concert on two strings instead of three, and Schoppert managed to extract the bolt during a long intermission.

The Festival has turned the burden of so many pianos to advantage in several ways. Each summer, apprentice tuners with at least a year of classroom instruction are trained on the practice pianos at the campus. The program has a long waiting list because it is small, and talented apprentices, useful to the Festival, are accepted back as often as they wish. As for the pianos, those not owned by the Festival undergo a curious recycling. All that arrive before concert season are new and most have been pre-sold to retail stores before they leave the factory. A piano fresh from the crate hasn't reached its optimum sound, but in Aspen it gets at least twelve hours' attention from tuners and a summer's worth of breaking in. At the end of the season, pianos are checked for damage, then swaddled in quilts, loaded into trucks headed in various directions and sold in stores across the country—often bearing the marketable cachet of having been "played at the Aspen Festival." Some of them over the years have been signed, on the plate that holds the strings, by such legendary performers as Lili Kraus, Victor Babin, Rosina Lhévinne, Alicia de Larrocha and Rudolph Firkušný, giving them further romance.

But before they leave town, these pianos are offered first for sale in Aspen. Only a dozen or so may sell each summer, but over the years Festival pianos have saturated the town and the valley, from residences to hotels to restaurants like the Crystal Palace dinner theater. "Three legged, like a thing in a riddle" according to poet James Merrill, a piano attains its richness through use and through nurture, less by repeated tunings than by voicing—that adjustment and refinement of the action, the felts, and the tension of the strings that opens vistas of shadings and moods—so that the piano is finally a prism for sound, refracting beats into timbres, emotional hues, the realization of long-considered pieces on a seasoned instrument. Bösendorfers from Vienna, Bechsteins from Germany, Steinways from New York, many of them full concert grands rather than parlor models, have proliferated over the years from the Festival. Schoppert claims that there are more pianos per capita in the Roaring Fork Valley than anywhere else in the world.

Large, numerous, fetishistic objects within Western culture, pianos receive the lion's share of in-house care and, barring mishap, smaller instruments are kept up by their owners. The Festival does employ a full-time luthier, who repairs and rebuilds string instruments and chronically has more work than she can handle. Otherwise, musicians in trouble must improvise fast, as trombonist Robert Biddlecome did in 1986. At the first rehearsal of the season, during a reading of *Petrouchka*, he pushed his chair back, perhaps forgetting that there was no barrier at the back of the risers, and keeled over onto his trombone. As Lee Ingram, then manager of the Tent, described it, "The trombone had major damage, a bent slide, a crunched bell—it looked like bad plumbing. He knew a great repairman in New York, had it back in two days, and actually played the concert with it."

Bob Schoppert's emergence as principal piano tuner, with two children following the family trade, was well-timed, for Kurt Oppens, the Festival's original tuner, began turning his talents in another direction. During the early years, concert programs consisted of single mimeographed sheets listing pieces and performers, with sometimes an announcement of later events to take place that night or the following day. In 1955 Norman Singer, knowing Oppens' background in musicology, asked him to provide some program notes. What Oppens provided and expanded over the years were not the usual rundowns of how a piece came to be written, or run-throughs of which theme followed which; they were shapely essays that ranged from history to musical structure to analogies with the current state of human affairs. Concertgoers began clipping their favorite notes from the programs and taping them onto their record albums, or tucking them into a collection of Oppens' notes that was published in 1975.

Part of the joy of Oppens' essays is that one can never predict their destination. A note on Hindemith's *The Four Temperaments*, for instance, opens with some historical linguistics, chronicles the music's emergence as a Balanchine ballet, and concludes—as if through Borgesian mirrors—to relate the piece to a tradition of "artful variational mazes" in which themes are themselves compounded variations, related as "one's niece, for instance, might be at the same time one's half-sister or one's cousin." A note on Berg will quote, in Oppens' own translation, from writings on Berg's musical structure, depict the evanescence of Berg's music as a gathering of mini-motifs that seem to revoke themselves before coalescing into a higher unity, then relate that revocation to a tradition initiated by Schubert that in turn reflects the blend of skepticism and Catholicism in Austrian popular drama—making the whole journey intelligible. There is no need to belabor the brilliance of these pieces; they merely need pointing out.

By doing his job so well Oppens created a monster, for the Festival eventually demanded a note—by Oppens or someone else—for every piece played, and eventually there were roughly two hundred pieces per summer. At first Oppens' notes were cut because of limited space, but later he was given free rein and could, he said, "write novels if I wanted." The constriction for program annotators is one of time, for the schedule of the pieces to be played is not finalized until April, there is only the spring to produce material and program writers are still working on the end of the season after it has started. "I could always do a good job on the first five weeks," said Oppens, "but had to write the last four in a rush." After so many years he amassed a backlog of pieces that could be reused, but felt compelled to expand, update, and square older notes with newer thinking. Oppens eventually let an assistant, Jane Jaffe, have her pick of pieces to write about that were not already covered, and occasionally he used the notes of others when he found material he respected or simply didn't like a piece. "It is unprofessional for an annotator to be influenced by his opinion of the music, but occasionally it happens."

Said Oppens of his attitude toward music, "I was always a non-player among performing musicians and I considered it my mission in life, since I was a teenager, to be an ear, so to speak, a listener. The listening I did in my best moments had nothing to do with what other people were doing, and I found no one with whom I could satisfactorily communicate my way of hearing. I tried to do it through my program notes." Oppens was always surprised when people actually referred to his ideas, believing that concertgoers skimmed or bypassed the notes entirely, but he persevered into his mid-eighties and upon his death, in 1998, he left the Aspen Music Festival a body of work from which it will be able to draw for the duration of its own life. Among other considerations, Oppens returned to the Festival a strand of what was lost when music separated from the Institute, and his notes connected musical feeling with the intellect in a manner that would have pleased a man who was as important to Kurt Oppens as to Walter Paepcke: Johann Wolfgang von Goethe.

Also Sprach Zara

JUST AS THE FESTIVAL had evolved from a small, select chamber program to six-orchestra nonstop music-making driven by a school that eventually topped one thousand students, so did the programming expand from the original core German repertoire plus Berlioz—who, in the words of Jorge Mester, was "only French by default"—to the full spectrum of Western classical music that comprised the eventual calendar. The divergence from the concentratedly German came early, with the split from Walter Paepcke and the influence of Darius Milhaud. Being a prominent composer, Milhaud's opinion was given the most weight, and he had a strong dislike for certain composers, beginning with Brahms and Tchaikowsky. Walter Susskind, who was music director in 1962 and again from 1964 to 1968, introduced unusual works by English composers, as well as Czech and other Middle European repertoires. Mester thought that French and Spanish music never got the full hearing they deserved—"I'm still trying to program Granados' *Goyescas*," he complained in 1988—but over the years the Festival has expanded its selections until its so-called Western music encompassed the five continents and numerous islands.

The area of greatest diversity may have been the contemporary program, which was co-managed by Darius Milhaud and Charles Jones until Milhaud's departure in 1968. Jones' composition classes were highly regarded and one of his string quartets won a Pulitzer Prize, but Milhaud remained, in the public's eye, the star. As a personality as well as a composer, Milhaud was controversial. Enthused Viviane Thomas, who studied voice with his wife Madeleine, "Darius was funny, as charming as charming can be. He was always relaxed, a little bemused, and there was tremendous affection between the two of them. They appreciated their students, brought us into their circle, and there was never any speaking down or condescension." As a conducting student James Conlon was enamored of the music, and when he knocked his glasses off twenty seconds into a performance of *La création du monde* in front of the composer, he conducted the rest from memory—not knowing until then that the music was in fact memorized—and made it a point to memorize all the scores he could thereafter.

Stuart Sankey was less keen on the composer. Sankey granted that Milhaud's early works had charm and wit, and that he did a beautiful setting of the Jewish Sabbath service, but believed that the standing ovations were due to his walking on and offstage with great difficulty, using two canes. The premieres of his works were dreaded by many, and after one of them Victor Gottlieb muttered, "We've done our annual performance of the emperor's new clothes." One Aspenite named her cat Darius Meow, after the composer's presumed caterwauling, and a subsequent female became, inevitably, Madeleine. There was, therefore, mixed anticipation of the 1957 premiere of Milhaud's *Aspen Serenade*, written for nine instruments as a tribute to the town and composed in five movements, one for each letter of the town's name. The piece was programmed for late August, but because it was to be a grand event the first reading was held in early July, the first of scheduled weekly rehearsals. Milhaud had expected to be congratulated on his triumph after the first run-through, but the work was greeted by the musicians in dead silence. The weekly rehearsals were canceled and the work wasn't taken up again until two days before the premiere. The audience found the piece interminable and meaningless, and remarked one concertgoer, referring to its five-movement format based on the five letters of Aspen, "I'm just glad we don't live in Garmisch-Partenkirchen." The piece was given a repeat and better-rehearsed hearing in 1992, but Milhaud the personality remembered by Viviane Thomas is recalled more fondly than the composer played by Gottlieb and Sankey.

From the departure of Milhaud in 1968 until 1985, new music was presented by Richard Dufallo, a Juilliard professor who conducted and socialized in his trademark cream jacket. The summer's contemporary offerings were presented during three successive Tuesdays in August, and many of the works were extensions of the tradition by such established composers-in-residence as Aaron Copland, Elliott Carter, Nicholas Nabokov, Jacob Druckman and Peter Maxwell Davies. But these were also the years of cultural rebellion, artistic outrage, the happening and musical neo-dada, and Dufallo's concerts drew, beyond a conventional following of music-lovers, a core of zealots who hoped to be, if not pleased, at least seriously offended. In the late sixties and early seventies, pianos were plucked and whacked on the tail, water glasses were bowed, cellos crooned mighty like whales and violas sounded like nightingales dying of nerve gas. There were trios for oboe, snare drum and tape deck. There were aleatory farts for brass. On one occasion a man in a karate suit ran screaming from the stage and beat a score of Chinese gongs that lined the Tent's perimeter. A staple was John Cage's music for prepared piano—of which George Shearing had run afoul— in which piano strings were outfitted with screws, washers, nuts and bolts so that a concert grand sounded like a Balinese gamelan orchestra, pieces so rarely played that pianist William Masselos wrote to Cage himself for the original hardware, the score and a set of instructions. The epoch's signature piece was the opera *Houdini*, by Peter Schat, part of the Conference on Contemporary Music during the 1980 season. A magician performed escape tricks in Paepcke Park the preceding week to drum up excitement and onstage props included a milk can from which Houdini himself had escaped. Near the end of the performance, during a séance in which Sir Arthur Conan Doyle attempts to communicate with the dead Houdini and the participants look up, expecting the voice of Houdini's ghost, the power snapped off, and with an unscripted flourish the opera concluded in the dark.

One Tuesday afternoon, percussionists sat on the stage in silence as if waiting for something to occur. Audience members, mystified, jumped out of their skins as a soprano shrieked and snapped finger bells directly behind them. The singer was Jan DeGaetani and the piece was Jacob Druckman's *Animus II*, a vocalized, drummed and acted drama about emotions between the sexes, from flirtation to rapture to rage. DeGaetani first appeared at the Festival in 1971 to sing George Crumb's *Ancient Voices of Children*, a piece she had commissioned that achieved a popularity rare for a new classical work. The following year there was an opening as well for her husband, English horn player Philip West, and they became permanent faculty. Until her death in 1989, DeGaetani drew many listeners who were otherwise wary of contemporary concerts but who appreciated her power and versatility, and as a teacher she fostered such talents as Renée Fleming, Dawn Upshaw and William Sharp. For the Festival she commissioned Richard Warnick's *Visions of Terror and Wonder*, which won the 1975 Pulitzer Prize for Music. Even though recordings of Festival concerts were not always up to marketing standards, there is a continuing commercial demand for DeGaetani's performances in Aspen.

Eventually the cutting-edge Tuesday afternoons were eliminated and new music was integrated with traditional programming, abolishing what Charles Jones called the "leper colonies" of all-contemporary concerts. Jorge Mester, with his background of recording contemporary music, was proud of integrating the new into popularly attended concerts, normalizing it—a practice that later music directors continued. Five contemporary violin works, for instance, were commissioned for five Dorothy DeLay alumni in honor of her seventy-fifth birthday in 1992, and premiered during Aspen Chamber Orchestra concerts over the course of two summers. Pre-concert lectures by the conductor, program notes, and the free "High Note" lectures every Wednesday noon at Paepcke Auditorium, often featuring visiting composers, help demystify these new sounds. The formal instruction pioneered by Charles Jones and Darius Milhaud has evolved into the Schumann Center for Composition Studies under Michael Czajkowski who, since the seventies, has run an electronic music studio for the Festival. Composition students using more traditional means have at their disposal the Aspen Contemporary Ensemble, consisting of violin, cello, flute, clarinet, piano and percussion, a scoring Schoenberg, omitting the percussion, used for *Pierrot lunaire* and which, in an unusual bit of conformity for the avant-garde, has been duplicated in hundreds of pieces since. Under the direction of George Tsontakis, who founded it in 1991, the core ensemble expands or contracts to perform works from the post-Schoenberg repertoire and offers readings of new compositions by Aspen students, an invaluable service for composers without other means of determining how their music sounds in performance. As a weekly highlight, every Saturday morning at the music campus, in a tiny building from the last century, a visiting composer will give an inside look at a recent composition, then submit to penetrating questions from the next generation of composers.

Besides the mixing of the old and the new, the Festival began adding an annual theme in 1970. Summer specialties have included Beethoven and his contemporaries, decadence as a musical force, love and death, the nine muses, music from Scandinavia, music from Australia, music from Hungary, music to commemorate the fiftieth anniversary of the end of World War II. For the summer theme in 1994, "Goethe and Music," for instance, the programming included Mahler's Eighth Symphony, which uses an extract from Goethe's *Faust* as a choral text; orchestral pieces from Berlioz's *Damnation of Faust*, and Wagner's *Faust* overture. The World War II commemoration included seldom heard works from the Terezin concentration camp, where artists were allowed to continue creating for a time before being exterminated. For three years the season ended with three-day all-day marathons: of Mozart in 1991, Beethoven in 1992 and Brahms in 1993. Not many composers can sustain this kind of allness and the marathons were dropped when the obvious composers had been celebrated.

A less conspicuous innovation involved a return to original ways of performing. As Mester described an approach to Beethoven, "To do the *Eroica* with a chamber orchestra is illuminating because we're so used to the Wagnerian sound of our gigantic orchestras, and the reduced forces are closer to the orchestra Beethoven used. Years ago I wanted to do the *Emperor Concerto* with the Chamber Symphony and was vetoed by everybody. Perceptions have changed. Critics have accused Beethoven of miscalculating the orchestration of the Fifth Symphony, but the real miscalculation is the thick orchestration that has been laid over the music since Beethoven's time. You can perform the piece perfectly well without doctoring the original orchestration, using the Chamber Symphony." Mester's Chamber Symphony performance of Beethoven's Fifth opened the 1985 season and those who attended out of duty, expecting a warhorse, found themselves hearing a crisper and more powerful symphony than the one they thought they knew.

An unofficial but persistent feature of the Festival has been the Big Piece—Bach's *St. Matthew Passion*, Haydn's *Creation*, Verdi's

Requiem, all with full orchestra plus chorus and soloists, or Strauss' *Alpine Symphony* with its twenty horn players. It was Jorge Mester's ambition to present all of the Mahler symphonies, a goal the Festival ultimately realized. Representative of the way such a piece can saturate a summer was the concert performance of Strauss's opera *Salome* in August 1988. The orchestra parts are so difficult that violist Nancy Thomas began rehearsing passages as soon as she arrived in June. A number of musicians listened to old recordings and some even read the Oscar Wilde text. One violinist so internalized the story of John the Baptist that she dreamt she was forced at gunpoint to behead her own son. For soprano Viviane Thomas it was the fulfillment of a dream. The final scene of *Salome* was one of the two pieces she learned simply because she adored them—"I'm mad for it," she exclaims, "and maybe Strauss was too, for it's the part of the opera he wrote first"—and she regularly used it as an audition piece, including when she was hired by the New York City Opera. She sang it for Mester the previous summer when he was considering programming *Salome* and he said he'd like to hear another part of it as well. "This is it," replied Thomas. "You like it or I'm not doing it." Mester liked it. George Shirley had sung the part of Herod in Spoleto in 1961, including two performances under assistant conductor Jorge Mester. "It's a frantic role," he recalls, "and duplicating it nearly three decades later and eight thousand feet high was a challenge."

"To learn the score was fantastic," said Thomas. "The beginning duet with Jokanaan turned out to be an inversion of the melodies. It was strange, fascinating, and I had to work it all out." She had her first rehearsal with Mester in New York, in December. "It's not unusual to rehearse a piece that far ahead. I think Jorge wanted to be sure I knew it." The first rehearsals in Aspen were rough, beginning with individual singers, then ensembles and finally principals and orchestra. Scott Morrison, a Kansas City psychiatrist who attends the Festival annually, went to all the rehearsals with the score. When he realized that Thomas was having trouble finding the first note of one of her entrances he went up to her, hoping he didn't sound presumptuous, and mentioned that her note was the last note that had been played by the violas. She thanked him for the clue and had no trouble finding the note in subsequent run-throughs. George Shirley was concerned that sun would beat on the Tent and leave him gasping for oxygen. The afternoon of the performance was blessed with clouds. Wanting to learn the music, Nadja Salerno-Sonnenberg played anonymously in the violin section, unrecognized by many of the fans who had jammed the tent to hear her two Sundays before. In the audience Viviane Thomas spotted an old friend she had seen only once in the last twenty years—the evening in New York when she had rehearsed with Mester—and she felt that many strands, musical and otherwise, were coming together at once. Not only did the performance conclude with a standing ovation and many bows, but afterward, said Thomas, people started asking her out. "'That was great,' they would say, 'how would you like to have dinner?' And I didn't even do the dance!"

For certain audience members, rehearsals such as those for *Salome* became even more interesting than performances. First locals, then visitors discovered Sunday morning orchestra rehearsals, when the afternoon program is often played through with scarcely a break. The soloist, being fresher, sometimes gives a freer performance, and the acoustics are more alive, either because cold air is a better conductor of sound or because there is less clothing and flesh to sop it up. Players dress in jeans, sweatshirts and T-shirts instead of formal black-and-whites and one timpanist, facing long stretches with nothing to play, spread the Sunday *New York Times* on top of his drums. Rehearsals, though serious, are leavened with a sense of play. When a guest conductor gestured the end of a chord, only to hear the top note continue, he rolled his eyes upward and muttered, "Plane in G." In 1975 Aaron Copland asked the orchestra to repeat the last chord of *Connotations for Orchestra,* a sustained dissonant blast. "Thanks," he said with a grin. "I just *love* making all that noise." Whenever Jorge Mester rehearsed, his dog Rags—a large mop punctuated with eyeballs and toenails—collapsed at his feet or sprawled against the pedals of the piano. Rags would sometimes submerge himself in the irrigation ditch that ran nearby, then follow his master into the Tent and shake, showering the stage. Said principal cellist Leopold Teraspulsky, "I was always a little worried about my cello being marred, but suing Jorge wouldn't exactly keep me my job."

Dogs aren't the only miscreants at rehearsals. Some visitors, perhaps thinking themselves timpanists, use the orchestra as background music for a rattling perusal of the Sunday paper, inciting one outraged regular to hiss at a woman clattering her way through *Arts & Leisure,* "Shall we ask the band to play more quietly so you can *read?*" When a man's wristwatch alarm went off, a piccolo player with perfect pitch joined in, followed by the entire wind section as the man shrank into his bench. A guest conductor rehearsed the applause-generating end to a movement, and the clapping that greeted every run-through demonstrated the Pavlovian trigger of the big finale. When intrusive applause for the same five bars finally diminished, the conductor turned to the audience and said, "I think you're getting it." Often conversation breaks out after rehearsal clapping, even though there are still phrases to refine, and when a frazzled conductor spun and yelled, "*Quiet,* we're trying to rehearse," an unfazed yapper shot back, "It's good enough!" Sunday morning tensions climaxed during a period when musicians' children ran the lemonade stand in slow motion and intermission scuffles developed as locals tried to beat musicians to the coffee. Frustrated players yelled, "Musicians first! This is a work break!" and their kids poured and counted change as if in a trance.

A group of Sunday morning regulars became Sergiu Comissiona cultists, eagerly awaiting his annual guest conducting, sit-

ting toward the side where they could best catch his manner of
leaning forward and sawing with the cellos, picking notes of the
piccolo out of midair, puffing his cheeks with the horns, advanc-
ing into the sound like a matador, then stepping back expectant-
ly and pointing to a soloist as if to say, "Do it!" The Comissiona
cabal also deliberated on Sundays over weekly clues to the iden-
tity of the *Aspen Times* music critic, usually someone recruited
from the Festival itself, writing under such pseudonyms as The
Syndicate and Phil S. Stein so as to avoid being felled from
behind by a sharpened bow. Some of the volunteer detectives
were *Times* reporters who watched the editorial office closely for
the arrival of unmarked manila envelopes and went so far as to
tail *Times* editor Bil Dunaway. A crucial suspect was once chal-
lenged to a round of Facts in Five to obtain a handwriting sample. All of the critics were eventually unmasked: one turned out
to be Jon Busch, a bassoonist who arrived with the Festival and
moved to Aspen; another was a Festival official; and a third,
exposed, refused to write further copy. Reviews were then permanently canceled and musicians returned to playing in a critic-
free environment: such was the intrigue that erupted when
Aspenites attended the Tent instead of church on Sunday morning. First free, then costing a couple of dollars, eventually requiring fees in the two figures to enter a rapidly filling Tent, Sunday
rehearsals at last became quasi performances—but an early dis-
coverer of the half-empty, music-filled canvas felt like George III
with a private orchestra playing for himself and his court.

Another event of growing popularity, less renowned than the
concert but open to the public, is the master classes. During the
Festival's first decades, posters announced the pieces in advance
so that those with relevant scores could bring them. No longer
divulged beforehand, these public lessons given by prominent
soloists and faculty members to their own and each other's students still provide a good way to learn the literature in depth,
offering new perspectives to those who play the pieces them-

selves and often giving more rounded exposure to young performers than formal recitals. Aware that students who are trying to learn and perform at the same time are under enormous pressure, the teachers are usually gentle and often humorous. Some over the years have also been idiosyncratic. One outspoken pianist lectured brilliantly at the beginning of each class on subjects as diverse as Mallarmé, Thomas Mann, the American Bicentennial, and the state of contemporary music; and once, to general astonishment, used his prologue to mock a composer-in-residence whose work he disapproved. Another teacher held forth for half an hour on people falling off piano benches while a student sat in terror of the Rachmaninoff prelude she never got to play. Itzhak Perlman's final master classes became so popular and brimming with jokes that the students may have received more instruction in how to handle crowds than how to phrase Mozart. But most master classes are serious work sessions, highlighted by such moments as when Lili Kraus was asked how someone with small hands could play big pieces, and the diminutive pianist replied, eyes flashing, "There are no small hands. There are only hands that think themselves small." Nor will those present forget when Rosina Lhévinne asked a young pianist to repeat the waltz from the slow movement of the Tchaikovsky concerto. "Certainly," he replied, "but what was wrong with it?" The answer impressed those aware that her husband had learned the piece from the composer and that she had probably heard it without relief for sixty years. "Nothing was wrong with it," she said. "You played it so beautifully I simply wanted to hear it again."

Master classes may sound esoteric to those who have not attended them, but they are underrated as popular entertainment, as well as a chance to hear performers in their own voices. In their comments, teachers display their own colorful natures, as witnessed by the following remarks heard over the years:

Phrase your notes, don't sound
like a typewriter gone mad.

It's just a retard, not a lunch break.

Must you land on the keys like a helicopter?

Smorzando, dear, that means get lost.

You played the Mozart so quietly that when you
tried to diminuendo, there was no place to go.
You can't shorten the pants unless you make them long.

In mock annoyance after an ovation held up the class:
*I **told** you not to play so well.*

After a Rachmaninoff concerto:
We have spent the summer trying to
distinguish between passion and violence.

One teacher didn't spare the coughing audience:
You guys sound like a catarrh concerto.

Various teachers, noting that piano fans always sit toward
the left, where they can watch the hands:
If this hall were a boat, it would capsize.

Besides instruction and entertainment, master classes can take
surprising turns. John Perry was once giving a master class in the
Wheeler Opera House to Yi Wu, who began playing piano during the Cultural Revolution in China when pianos were being
smashed. His father managed to build one in secret from scrap
parts. When there was a political opening, Yi Wu and his family
migrated to Argentina and then the United States, but funding
had come to an end and he was facing a return to China. Aspenite Goodrich Taylor, knowing nothing of this story, was so
impressed with his playing that she went backstage after the master class and asked Yi Wu if he needed financial help. She wound

up supporting his career, he attended college in the United States, and in 1993 he won the International Piano Competition in Calgary, Alberta.

Master classes are robustly attended by the public, but little known to the outside world was an annual event that took place for years at the Music Campus: Zara Nelsova's Deportment Lecture, alternatively known as *Also sprach Zara*. Nelsova was known for her extravagant full-length peach, burgundy and emerald gowns and a grandly gracious stage presence, as well as her cello playing, and her lectures added another facet to a glamorous persona. Consisting of hilarious stories told at her own expense, followed by morals, they targeted women cellists but their principles applied to musicians in general. She would begin with an ill-fated performance of the Boccherini Concerto when she was wearing a dress of high-neck but see-through netting, displaying cleavage. Near the end of the piece, the dress split and she was playing topless. She always carried an all-purpose drape for emergencies, and during the first moment when the orchestra played alone, she tossed it across her shoulders. When she stood to bow, the stool turned out to be resting on the bottom of the dress, completing the rip and splitting the dress down the side, so that she was forced to hobble off the stage with the cloth in one hand and the cello in the other and had to skip the curtain calls. Assorted morals: clothing, including shoes, socks and wrinkles in fabric, carry visually across the hall as surely as notes carry aurally; attend to what you're wearing. When your gown comes back from the dry cleaner, check for broken zippers and incipient rips. Never wear sheer fabrics or strapless gowns. Never play the cello with your knees on display; wear long skirts, preferably full-length gowns, with petticoats if necessary.

There followed two stories with a common message. Once during the Elgar, her pearls started slowly sliding off her neck and into her cleavage. After the scherzo she motioned to the conductor to stop, slowly drew the pearls out and handed them with great display to the concertmaster, who slipped them into his pocket, then signaled the conductor to continue. On another occasion a string broke and she said to the audience, "You'll have to excuse me, I just snapped a g-string." She had no idea why the audience howled, but once she found out, she always said she'd broken her g-string, no matter which string had actually snapped. Moral: if you can't mask a problem, turn it into a joke that includes the audience.

She concluded with general advice, unconnected to stories. No unnecessary tuning between movements. Tap the strings with your bow to see if they are out of tune, and if they are, adjust them quickly, softly and discreetly. No private jokes with other players during performance. Keep the end pin of your cello sharp; file it before you play in public. Dress in colors that fit the music; she preferred yellow for Debussy, red for Brahms and Dvořák. Keep your eyes down during the first bow. During the second bow you can look up a bit and glance at your audience. On the third bow you can hold your head up and gaze out.

It is unknown how much of this advice was taken, but students always left the deportment lecture in high spirits.

Sour Notes

THE STABILITY OF A FESTIVAL that had managed to invent itself, expand its school and its nine-week array of concerts, acquire a campus and even overcome the annual housing crisis would seem to have warded off the constant surprise that characterized the early years but, as Aristotle has pointed out, it is entirely probable that many improbable things should happen. In 1980 the Aspen Festival Orchestra was bused to the tundra up Independence Pass so they could be filmed, by helicopter, playing in a mountain meadow for a John Denver television special. To avoid exposing valuable instruments to the elements, the players were issued wooden replicas of everything from fiddles to bassoons, and such was the cold that everyone wore extra clothing beneath their concert black-and-whites, lending the orchestra a distinctly puffy look. Because no sound was being recorded, players freely exchanged instruments and the concertmaster was an oboist who had no idea how to hold a violin. Music recorded at their most recent concert was switched on loud so that the players could mime their playing in sync while a strapped-in cameraman leaned precariously out of a helicopter that swooped past them. The zaniness of the event so overcame the musicians afterward that they machine-gunned each other with the bassoons, then stuck a cello by its pin into the tundra and threw rocks at it. At two hundred dollars apiece for many it was their highest paying gig to date, and the entire exploit was reduced to thirty seconds of the show's introduction.

In 1995, as Gil Shaham ended the second movement of a Dvořák Violin Sonata, a man seated to the left and near the front asked Shaham in a loud voice to stand more to the side so he could see the keyboard. "I must be putting on weight," cracked Shaham with aplomb, then plunged into the third movement. There was much hilarity backstage during intermission but Debbie Ayers, the Festival's publicity director, who had been turning pages for the pianist, Gil's sister Orli, said she was surprised at the viciousness with which the offended audience turned on the man. When Shaham returned to the stage after intermission, he looked at the spot where the man had objected, moved his music stand far to the side, then returned it to its place, to much audience laughter. But the man wasn't there.

For the last concert of the 1988 season, Yefim Bronfman was scheduled to play Brahms' Piano Concerto No. 2 but was sick, and it wasn't known whether he could perform. Misha Dichter had gotten a call the day before the concert, asking him to show up for the Sunday morning rehearsal so he could run through the piece as a possible substitute, but he hadn't touched the music in months, was officially on vacation, and declined. On the day of the concert, Dichter went to brunch with friends, drank stiff bloody marys until three-thirty, and reached the Tent at a quarter to four to discover panic backstage; Bronfman was indeed sick, leaving the afternoon's other piece, Stravinsky's *Rite of Spring*, as the only music. Dichter was curious about how the Festival would handle the situation, sneaked onto the stage and hid on a chair behind the percussion for a discreet view. An announcer apologized to the audience for the cancellation of the Brahms, and Dichter, to his horror, had been spotted. The crowd began chanting Mee-sha! Mee-sha! As Dichter slumped further in his chair, Mayor Bill Stirling ran to the stage and shouted, "You can do it, Misha! You can do it!" Out of practice, unrehearsed and addled by vodka, Dichter knew better than to make a fool of himself and disappeared backstage until the Stravinsky was safely underway.

In 1996, when the summer theme was "Music and Nature," nature jumped the gun by releasing a May mudslide onto the music campus, burying four cars, slamming into the doors of the practice rooms and piling as high as eight feet on one corner of the Music Hall with boulders and splintered pine trees in a matrix of muck. That fiasco was at least reparable but another, during the summer of 1977, proved tragic. During the intermission of a Friday night Chamber Symphony concert the Tent was struck by a volley of gunfire. One concertgoer was killed and another injured. As principal second violinist Nancy Hill, who was inside the Tent, described it, "Bullets started zinging through the tent, actually ricocheting off the poles and the concrete floor. There was a lot of screaming outside. We just got down on the floor. The people socializing outside the tent listening came rushing in, and since the Cold War was still on I actually thought the Russians had attacked and we were under siege. The shots seemed to go on for a long time. Marty Verdrager, Tom Eirman, Bill Vickery and Jorge Mester were seized with adrenaline attacks and started running from the tent in four directions with no regard for their own safety." The Festival officials found that two boys were target practicing and had no idea where their bullets were going.

Despite such unforeseeable events, as it matured and stabilized through the decades, the Festival *was* more predictable, though the color didn't die all at once. During the 1960s Leopold Teraspulsky still worried that he would be held up on his way to the Tent because of sheep drives, when Basque shepherds on horseback, assisted by dogs, clogged the streets as they herded their flocks through town to summer pastures on Aspen Mountain. In the 1970s oboist Deborah Barnekow camped with eight other students in a meadow between the music campus and town, being careful not to rouse the night watchman when they sneaked into the business office at night to cadge showers.

In 1979 it was still possible for a faculty member to get into trouble. When Elliott Carter was composer-in-residence, he and his wife stayed in a Victorian across from Timothy Marquand, a piano student of Edith Oppens. Marquand held Carter in awe and decided to show his appreciation by inviting the Carters on an end-of-the-season all-day jeep trip. "I had been reading too many portentous program notes on Carter's work," says Marquand. "I told him, 'I will show you mountains to match your music.'" The Carters were in their seventies but Marquand figured them to be citizens of the world who didn't need coddling and he arranged an adventurous loop through Redstone, over Scofield Pass to Crested Butte, then over Pearl Pass back to Aspen. He lined up an experienced driver who picked up the party in an open jeep. The Carters "carried light sweaters in case of a slight chill and were otherwise dressed for a 'twenties Riviera picnic." They rode in good style up treacherous Scofield Pass, spread a cloth, lunched on bread, cheese and wine while admiring the view from a high meadow, and Marquand considered himself "on top of the world with some of its top people." They descended to Crested Butte and Marquand stopped at a gas station not to tank up, merely to ask the condition of Pearl Pass. "I just drove it yesterday," assured the attendant. "It's clear sailing."

When they reached the top of the pass they found it deeply snowed in: the attendant had lied. They didn't have enough gas to return to Crested Butte, they couldn't go forward and the sun was setting. Marquand dispatched the driver to run toward Ashcroft for help while he walked the Carters over the pass. As the Carters proceeded over the snow in low-cut sneakers, Marquand had visions of helicopters, searchlights and Gordon Hardy. At one point Mrs. Carter said, "Oh look, Elliott, there's a grouse," and she began to follow it.

"Stay on the road, Helen," replied Carter. "The road *knows*."

As they began to descend, the last sun lit up a ridge and Carter remarked, "Zarathustra has walked here." Marquand's immediate goal was Taggart Hut, a refuge for climbers. At one point Marquand asked Carter, "What would Copland do in a situation like this?"

Replied Carter, "Aaron would sit down."

They reached the hut at nightfall to find two Germans brewing soup. Marquand left the Carters happily chatting in German with the mountaineers and ran down the dark road, to be met by the oncoming headlights of "a hippie VW bus the driver had commandeered." Marquand and the driver actually managed to get the Carters safely to their Victorian by bedtime and they flew off to Paris at six the next morning.

Despite such adventures, as the Festival grew and solidified, complaints began to surface that much of the flavor had been lost because no one had free time. The addition of Monday night chamber concerts was greeted by some musicians the way Monday night football was greeted by some sports fans: too much of a good thing. Herta Glaz, who returned to teach at the Festival in the late 1987, dismissively referred to the fold-out concert calendar full of fine print as "the map." Recalled Nancy Thomas, "When I first came here there were only three concerts a week and everybody went to everything. Faculty went to student recitals. How could that happen now?" Said Adele Addison, "Music has content and you have to absorb and reflect—you can't do that if you're off to the next event. Some like the fact that you can pick and choose and don't have to go to everything. But back when it was three times a week you *wanted* to go to everything. There was something special about concerts, and now we're very definitely a school."

A corollary to wall-to-wall programming was the loss of time for other activities. Because of the size and workload, Monday all-Festival picnics had become distant memories. Musicians no longer had free evenings when they could gather in each other's houses to read through scores. Three-day faculty backpacks were gone by the mid-seventies and even dayhikes started becoming problematic. Nights when the Festival parodied itself were also gone, for music was now not only fulltime; it was fulltime serious. Cipa Dichter worried about her teacher, Aube Tzerko: "He was paler at the end of the summer than when he arrived. It was terrific for his students, but when did he get to recharge his batteries?" From the nearby Aspen Center for Physics, where most of the time is still unplanned, the Music Festival looked particularly frantic, and physicist Paul Fishbane gave up on bringing his violin to Aspen because Festival musicians lacked the time to play with him.

Students had their own grievances. The six eventual orchestras were created so that all students could have orchestral experience, with a variety of options—but some in training for solo careers resented the incursion on their time. In the diagnosis of pianist Jackie Melnick, "You get into this bind that you need scholarship money for students, and to get it you need more performances, and for that you need more orchestras, and finally you have so many orchestras to bring in audiences that you're not doing what you want for the students. Many of them play in orchestras all winter, and in the summer they want to escape that regimen and do solo or chamber playing. Students leave Aspen with no new solo repertoire because they spent their whole time in orchestras, and orchestras don't make you a better musician. Of course that's specifically a string problem—with winds and horns, their careers are made in orchestras." The leading string teacher, on the other hand, Dorothy DeLay, believed that all violinists should be trained as soloists even if their career destination was the orchestra, and her school-within-a-school devoted itself to individual careers. Cloyd Duff, who had played with the Festival Orchestra in 1966 and returned during the eighties to teach, put his finger on the problem. "You give students new ideas but they don't have time to take them in. Their reason for coming to Aspen is to absorb private lessons under the guidance of a teacher, but they're too busy running from one event to another. They can't assimilate their instruction until the season's over, and by then they've forgotten half of it."

The upshot of so much orchestra playing was witnessed by Lee Ingram, tent manager during the mid-1980s, who regularly had to subtract seats for absentees. "A lot of kids didn't show up for the Festival Orchestra. There was no problem with the winds, who are principal players, but strings took it less seriously. What was the Festival going to do—expel you after you'd paid your tuition? Some kids wondered what the point was of playing twelfth stand cello." Arranging seating for less visible functions, former tech crew member Bert Lewis found that some student recitals were virtually unattended. "I set up chairs for events and there was no one to listen. I moved pianos for recitals and no one came." It was seldom the case that students had gone fishing or into the hills, as might have been true earlier in the Festival; most resembled conducting student James Conlon, who allowed himself only one excursion during his first summer, a gondola ride during which he remarked, "This is like Central Park," and nearly got pitched off of Aspen Mountain. Students were working on their technique more than ever, but there were so many public events—and so many other students—that many slipped out to practice on their own.

For a time, students were conscripted for another duty beyond their fields of study—to sing in the chorus. For those with the time and inclination, the experience was enriching, and when conducting students were drafted to sing in Mahler's Resurrection Symphony under Walter Susskind, Conlon was thrilled to participate, to learn the piece from the inside. There was even a minor tradition of wellknown players performing anonymously, typified by Nadja Salerno-Sonnenberg, who played violin with the orchestra in Verdi's *Requiem*, French horn in a William Bolcom fanfare, and plans to play trumpet if the Bolcom is repeated. A keen eye on the Verdi *Requiem* would also have spotted pianist Claude Frank singing in the chorus. But medium-crossover is better if voluntary. One August in the early seventies, all keyboard students were required to sing in the chorus of Berlioz's *The Damnation of Faust.* Many resented the daily infringement on piano practice, cut singing rehearsal, or declined to raise their voices. A threat by the conductor John Nelson to cancel the performance brought the piece together—gloriously, but at the last minute, under pressure and after intoning, "The only salvation is good diction." The choral duties have now been professionalized by the Colorado Symphony Chorus and Colorado Children's Chorale, but for awhile compulsory singing cut into the time of students who were vocal only in their objections.

Carping didn't end with overscheduling; it extended to what was seen as ever more popular programming. Representative comments over the years include Mary Norris: "Before we never played Tchaikovsky symphonies. It's the popcorn-and-peanut crowd. They're catering to the Sunday audience." Stuart Sankey: "Under Norman Singer we would never do *Pines of Rome,* never do a Hollywood Bowl type of repertoire. Now it's box office." Kurt Oppens: "I'm not always in agreement with the pieces that are chosen as crowd pleasers. The *Organ* Symphony of Saint-Saëns is to me, for instance, a perfect horror and it's been played twice in the last two years. I'm afraid my hatred of Carl Orff's beloved *Carmina Burana* even infected my note, which is unprofessional." Zara Nelsova: "When I was first here I did the Hindemith, Barber and Milhaud concertos, and Bloch's *Schelomo.* I wanted to do the Dvořák, but Norman Singer wouldn't let me. Aspen was not for that repertoire, he told me. Now that's all they want me to play." When Nelsova was scheduled to play Grieg's melodic but critically disesteemed cello sonata, Oppens turned over the note on the piece to another writer and at the last minute Nelsova substituted a Brahms. Jorge Mester took a caustic pride in introducing works whose familiarity had made them taboo. "It was the summer of Woodstock and I heard David

The Festival grew from the efforts of Chicago-industrialist Walter Paepcke and his wife, Elizabeth, who were looking to establish a cultural center in a mountain setting. (*Ferenc Berko/ Photographers Aspen*)

Opera singers Jerome Hines and Herta Glaz at home on the range. (*Ferenc Berko/Photographers Aspen*)

oncert-goers line up for tickets to the Saarinen Tent. (*Ferenc Berko/Photographers Aspen*)

Igor Stravinsky was the first composer to conduct his own works at Aspen. (*Ferenc Berko/ Photographers Aspen*)

Nathan Milstein and Gregor Piatigorsky perform in the tent as Dimitri Metropoulos conducts the orchestra during the Goethe Bicentennial. (*Ferenc Berko/ Photographers Aspen*)

omposer Peter Schickele (left) became famous for his humorous creation PDQ Bach, a character
e invented while a student at Aspen. French composer Darius Milhaud (right) established the
onference on Contemporary Music and stayed sixteen summers. (left: *Charles Abbott/Photog-
phers Aspen;* right: *Ferenc Berko/Photographers Aspen*)

aron Copland once asked the orchestra to repeat the last chord of *Connotations for Orchestra*,
sustained dissonant blast. "Thanks," he said with a grin. "I just love making all that noise."
Charles Abbott/Photographers Aspen)

Some audience members especially enjoyed the expressive gestures of guest conductor Sergiu Comissiona. (*Charles Abbott/Photographers Aspen*)

James Levine, who went on to a spectacular career as artistic director of the Metropolitan Opera, first came to Aspen as a fourteen-year-old student and spent fifteen summers there. (*Charles Abbott/Photographers Aspen*)

Zara Nelsova's annual deportment lectures, highlighted by her amusing first-hand stories of what not to wear while performing, were always popular with students. (*Charles Abbott/Photographers Aspen*)

egendary violin teacher Dorothy DeLay reviews a score with Midori, one of her many star ͻpils. Shuttling between Juilliard and Aspen, DeLay has had an astonishing number of students ͻ on to internationally acclaimed solo careers. (*Charles Abbott/Photographers Aspen*)

Lawrence Foster came to Aspen as a student and went on to become the Festival's music direct◌
for six years, 1991–1996. (*Charles Abbott/Photographers Aspen*)

Popular entertainer John Denver sits between Edgar Stern (left), who is a former chairman of th◌
board, and Gordon Hardy, the Festival's former president and dean. (*Charles Abbott/Photo◌
raphers Aspen*)

zhak Perlman and Jorge Mester share a light moment during rehearsal. (*Charles Abbott/
hotographers Aspen*)

n playing in front of so many other musicians, long-time Festival regular Misha Dichter ad-
tted, "Nothing is scarier than playing in Aspen. Your colleagues are there and you want to play
ll." (*Charles Abbott/Photographers Aspen*)

Kurt Oppens (left) came to Aspen as a piano tuner but soon turned to writing the Festival program notes. His elegant essays were cherished by concert-goers. Pinchas Zukerman (right) sit in with students playing for donations, a familiar summer tradition in the streets and restaurant of Aspen. (left: *Ferenc Berko/Photographers Aspen*; right: *Charles Abbott/Photographers Aspen*)

Another one of Dorothy DeLay's students, Nadja Salerno-Sonnenberg came to Aspen as a you girl and now regularly returns each summer to perform. (*Charles Abbott/Photographers Aspen*)

Zinman conduct the Tchaikovsky Sixth on the radio. I thought it was terrific and asked him to repeat it in Aspen. Its programming provoked a letter from Elizabeth Paepcke, who said I had 'trampled on the philosophy of the Festival.' So you can hold me responsible for the crumbling of taste."

During the Mester tenure there was a rule that five years had to elapse before a piece could be repeated, but afterward certain pieces seemed to recur nearly annually. For orchestral works, the rationale is that students need to learn the standard repertoire as well as esoterica, and to disallow what some might deem war horses would deprive them of essential experience in what is, ultimately, a more orchestral than solo-driven musical world. The average student participation in Aspen is three summers, and the five-year rule against repeats would keep many from experiencing core repertoire. *Rite of Spring* was performed three times during the nineties, but by three different orchestras in an effort to balance the needs of students with audience taste. Disagreements about programming can probably be reconciled by the sheer scope of the summer program, large enough to offer lots of the popular, lots of the arcane.

Complaints among faculty and students about scheduling, repertoire and the like were nothing compared to the pitched battle, wholly invisible to the public, between Festival director Gordon Hardy and non-musician board members, climaxed by the resignation of twenty-two trustees at once. Such dissension was hardly new. At a meeting of the administrative board during the fifties, two absent members, violinist Roman Totenberg, who was chair of the administrative committee, and conductor Izler Solomon, were fired by the others. The board of trustees knew nothing about it and was horrified. Said Kurt Oppens, "I would rather not have a festival than hurt people to the extent those two were hurt." On the other hand, Solomon had been, in Stuart Sankey's words, "mean-spirited, rude at rehearsals and incompetent at conducting. One summer he was told that if his behavior with the orchestra didn't improve, he would be dismissed. His behavior persisted and the following summer we had meetings with committees and trustees, and he was finally let go." On another occasion Rosina Lhévinne couldn't play a Mozart concerto because of illness, Jeanine Dowis was substituted, and a faculty furor ensued over whether Dowis was qualified. Over the years, regular faculty members had not been invited back simply because age had taken its toll on their playing or teaching, or there were personality problems, the sheer operation of a large Festival necessarily generating the occasional hard feeling.

Attempts had been made to head off problems structurally. After musicians took over the administration of the Festival in 1954, in the wake of the Leach affair, power had been divided between an administrative committee, composed of musicians, and a board of trustees, with no clear lines of authority. The Festival was proclaimed a two-headed monster and labor arbitrator Nate Feinsinger, a summer resident and Festival-goer, was brought in to restructure it. The resulting arrangement has evolved over the years, but basically the Festival has been run by a corporation of two hundred members, divided equally between musicians and non-musicians. Within the corporation is a group of up to fifty trustees, eleven of whom are musicians. The function of the trustees is to raise money, guide the organization financially, and make donations themselves. Trustees may propose changes in the bylaws, but the corporation as a whole must vote on them, and it is within the corporation that disagreements have been played out.

Controversy erupted when Gordon Hardy, who had been dean of students and then executive director of the Festival, also became president of the organization. Hardy's detractors, who continued to give him high praise for his artistic direction, criticized his handling of financial powers the new position gave him. He had brought in new foundation grants and secured well-known artists for a fraction of their normal fees—then seemed reckless in the spending of that same money. Unauthorized by the board, he sent an orchestra to the Mostly Mozart Festival and lost money. He refused to divulge the salaries and housing allowances of faculty. Still less to the board's liking was his insistence on staging the opera *Houdini*, which generated the kind of publicity that couldn't be bought but which lost almost fifty thousand dollars. Hardy never gave the board a full accounting; on the other hand, it was known that he paid the debts out of his own pocket.

As the situation polarized over several years, Hardy's defenders, primarily musicians, said that the board of trustees cared only for finance and was trying to meddle in artistic affairs; by not understanding that musicians will accept smaller fees in return for artistic control, they would wind up with a smaller Festival of expensive artists, or no Festival at all. The anti-Hardy forces, primarily fundraising non-musicians, complained that Hardy couldn't communicate, sought power, and misled musicians by falsely alleging that trustees wanted to interfere in artistic decisions. They declared themselves unwilling to fundraise for a Festival being led into debt. Said Jeanne Jaffee, who served, in 1981–82, as the Festival's only woman chair of the board to that point, "You would write Gordon a letter and he would answer or not. If he did, you would never get an answer to your question, you would get esoteric nonsense. You could never pin him down. You can't imagine the frustration of working with Gordon." In Hardy's counter-assessment, "Recent controversy has been about none of the things I deem important, which are quality and artistic matters. The controversy is about what's less important—power—and I'm dealing with human nature. Don't expect me to watch the Festival disintegrate after we've built it up for so many years. If there's a place like this that's doing better, I don't know about it. If I had any weaknesses that were obvious to me, I'd be working on them. I don't evaluate myself—I just try to do the best I can."

The jockeying of pro- and anti-Hardy forces was waged, as prescribed, within the corporation. Trustees made proposals to curtail Hardy's financial powers, then the corporation at large altered bylaws to retain them. Tensions exploded in August 1985 when the corporation further expanded Hardy's power by making him chief executive officer. The board believed that its own chair, W. Ford Schumann, was the logical choice for CEO. Schumann resigned in protest of Hardy's elevation, followed a week later by twenty-two of the thirty-five board members, including all of those who had been with the Festival from the beginning except James Hume. Said Jaffee of the mass exit, "It wasn't coordinated, it was a happening. Gordon refused everything that was asked, and we all got up and left." Hardy did not find the walkout so spontaneous. In his own version, there was much commentary against him, then during a break a board member took him aside and advised him to resign, for three board members had telephoned the trustees and committed twenty-two of them to walking out. Sensing the integrity of the Festival threatened by plotters, Hardy stood his ground, and the choreographed happening proceeded. Among those who resigned was Elizabeth Paepcke, who explained, "It's the board that has to raise money. We told Gordon he had to have a business manager with equal stature to himself, and a president of the board above both of them. It's the way any orchestra is run. Gordon wouldn't have it."

Fritz Benedict, who hadn't been strongly identified with either faction but had occupied himself with solving the housing problem, was brought in as the new chair. Replacement board members were quickly found. In Benedict's summation, "I have some sympathy with the trustees who left, because Gordon hadn't handled the situation too well. But the trustees thought they could let it fold and bring up a new Festival from the ashes. I don't think it's that easy to do."

There were, in any case, no ashes. Even a regular concertgoer who was not tuned into Festival gossip would have missed the earthquake, and Hardy remained at his post just inside the entrance to the Tent, standing and serene, until his retirement in 1989. For his farewell concert, Viviane Thomas fulfilled a Straussian dream to follow her *Salome*. "I had always wanted to sing the *Four Last Songs*, in the way there are places you want to see once in your life. To do so for Gordon's last concert was very emotional. It took all my concentration, because it wasn't just the pieces. It was the occasion."

When Music
Is in Tents

GORDON HARDY HAD DIRECTED the Festival for twenty-eight of its fifty years, and transfer of his position to Robert Harth was another example of generational change within the Festival itself, for Harth had begun his career as a Festival brat. Son of violinist Sidney Harth, his first position was guardian of a tent flap at the age of eight. He worked for twelve summers with the tent crew, became general manager of the Los Angeles Philharmonic and managing director of the Hollywood Bowl, then returned to Aspen as a Festival Director who still recognized trucks he had driven as an employee. The following year Jorge Mester, who had served as music director for twenty years—longer by several multiples than any other conductor—was replaced by Aspen alumnus Lawrence Foster. Having studied piano in Aspen, audited the conducting class of Izler Solomon, roomed with composition student William Bolcom, and played piano at Mario's (Aspen's fondly remembered restaurant with singing waiters), before conducting the Houston Symphony and the Monte Carlo Orchestra, Foster was steeped in Aspen traditions. These changes were a matter of extending the Festival legacy and, in Harth's case, adding infrastructure, beginning with an alternate concert facility to the Tent.

To understand the latter, it is necessary to know more about the Tent itself. Used for rehearsals when there are no concerts, the Tent is scheduled from eight in the morning until midnight and may be the busiest concert hall in the United States during its period of operation. A chamber concert may include five or six groups, some of whom may want three or four rehearsals for the concert. In 1986, for instance, there were seventy-six concerts and 256 rehearsals spread over the nine weeks, and while the orchestra rehearsals and concerts were set beforehand, the rest of the rehearsal time had to be negotiated with the tent manager. Keeping the schedule book straight is a major undertaking. Lee Ingram, who arrived in 1980 as a horn student and played in the Festival Orchestra before becoming tent manager, calculated that even with assistants he averaged a sixty-hour work week.

In describing his job, Ingram said, "I was responsible for facility maintenance, everything from cleaning the stage and bathrooms, taking out the dead rats in the morning that the cats brought in—it happened—to tending the tent proper, the canvas." But custodial duties were the easy part, and Ingram found more of his energies spent as negotiator. "People got into conflicts about how much time they needed for rehearsal, and there were always a few who thought they deserved extra. Some came in with the attitude that you have to establish your authority by complaining, which doesn't play well in the West. Pianists griped the most. On the other hand the Emerson Quartet, for instance, was great, not neurotic at all, and ceded a bunch of time because they figured they already knew what playing in the tent was like. There have been difficult seasons and others, like 1988, that were almost magic in terms of people deferring to each other to work the time out."

Time was only one of the coordinates that Ingram had to manage; the other was space. Charts of the stage, known as set-up sheets, had been printed so that the configuration of the orchestras could be blocked in ahead of time. Explained Ingram, "The stage is an odd shape, and they tend to jam so much on it. It's impossible for someone else to remember, so I assigned sections to each of the staff, then adjusted everything. With the Festival Orchestra you had twenty-two first violins, twenty seconds, only thirty minutes between Chamber Symphony and Festival Orchestra rehearsals, and you had to get it seatable right away. Having played in the orchestra helped, knowing what instruments were in a certain piece, but some of the hands didn't even know what a violin was, let alone how to seat people, and they had to be trained." A TV monitor showing the performance area allowed Ingram to make sure from backstage that the orchestra was correctly seated and the soloist was happily situated. The monitor came into play again at the end of the piece, the point when the doors open as if by premonition for exiting conductor and soloist, though there were occasions when a backstage well-wisher blocked the screen and a soloist banged into a door.

Also, there was human nature. "A lot of students thought they were part-time stage hands," said Ingram, "and we had to tell them, we have percussion and harps coming behind you, and you're going nowhere unless you discuss it with the harpist." He was amused when a group of students brought marshmallows to toast in the heaters, but had to level with a staff person who asked for four times his allotment of rehearsal time, brought food, drink and his dog among expensive instruments, and finally got told that the crew couldn't be stepping on salami sandwiches while setting up for the next group.

One would assume that the order of pieces on a program is arranged for artistic balance, but again the set-up must always be considered—a point best illustrated by a concert gone wrong. "It was a nightmare of a contemporary concert," recalled Ingram, "going from two pianos and six percussions to a string quartet to a thirty-five-piece orchestra. It's hard enough to get and hold an audience for contemporary anyway, and this was a two-and-a-half hour concert, half of which was taken up by changes. We didn't even bother with a formal intermission. Needless to say, there was hardly anybody left at the end. We always tried to avoid that by planning, so that complicated maneuvers, including rearranging the baffles, were handled during intermission."

Audience members unaware of the organization required to produce music in the Tent would certainly be startled to learn that a fellow concertgoer, a veteran of the Merchant Marines knowledgeable about the effects of wind on canvas, was responsible for installing the bellow ropes and voluntarily checking them every summer. In 1988, ten minutes before a concert during which Nadja Salerno-Sonnenberg was to play the Barber Concerto to the biggest house of the summer, a thirty-second gust of wind had the Tent flailing. As Ingram described the scene, "Somebody came up to me and said, 'Lee, you'd better see this.' There was a rip in a panel. Bellow ropes are attached to the midpoints of the panels to keep them from flapping, and the middle of each panel is fastened to a steel cable. Because of the differential between the gale on the outside and the reduced pressures on the inside, the tent acts as a huge sail, which is why it flaps in the wind. The steel cable had snapped, but the bellow rope was still holding. If you actually shred a panel, the wind could whip it into the tent and we were ready to get on the P.A. system and clear out the section. Fortunately the wind died down after the one blast and very few people knew. The guy from the Merchant Marines came running backstage to assure me we could proceed. By the time people were filing out of the tent, we were up on ladders, fixing it."

Interacting with the tent crew, but moving equipment and preparing rehearsals and concerts at the campus and all over town, is the tech crew. Both average seven members. Starting a month before the Festival, the tech crew moves out the Aspen Country Day School, a private secondary school that occupies the music campus during the winter, and moves the Festival in. They raise the Tent and install the lighting and sound equipment inside.

They receive and uncrate the pianos, move them around town during the summer and recrate them afterward. During the season they set up for rehearsals and concerts at the campus and remain on site to field anything that goes amiss. Night duty involves making sure all students have left the campus by eleven P.M., then doing set-ups for the morning, which can last until one A.M.—though that time, according to ex-tech member Bert Lewis, also involves "a lot of watching TV, driving around in the trucks and raiding the cafeteria."

Ranging farther afield than the tent crew, the tech crew has more competitive disaster stories. During Tim Willoughby's tenure as tent manager during the 1970s, the truck with Fernando Valenti's harpsichord fell into a river and the instrument had to be shipped to New York for rebuilding. On another occasion Willoughby found that kids had sneaked into the Tent, discovered the piano rigged with nuts and bolts for one of the ever problematic Cage pieces, took it for a joke in bad taste and nearly made off with the hardware before they were stopped. Bert Lewis's initiation into tech crew snafus occurred during his first summer at age eighteen, when an elevator door in the Aspen Square building kept banging shut on a piano they were trying to move out, opening and slamming it until Lewis managed to crawl underneath and punch an alarm button that stopped the door. When they wheeled the piano to the waiting pianist's apartment, eighteen keys had been knocked out and Bob Schoppert had to remove the action and perform heroic surgery. At the end of a later season when they had moved pianos all summer with nary a nick, they gathered the pianos on their sides in an evenly spaced row in the campus Music Hall to ready them for their crates, knocked one over, and fourteen fell like dominoes onto their lids. The instruments were insured, but the hundred dollar deductible on each added up to fourteen hundred dollars.

The tech crew competed in a running practical joke war with the tent crew. After the tent crew tried to bind the boss of the tech crew with duct tape, the boss of the tech crew baked a box of brownies with six boxes of laxative and sent them to the tent crew with a spurious thank-you note from a departing musician. During the seventh week of every season, when all are getting tired, the tent and tech crews have an annual tug-of-war over an Aspen Institute pond so that the losing team always gets wet.

The real tug-of-war at the center of all this frenzy has been the Tent itself, with its colorful audience that is, for the musicians, *their* show. Audiences have luxuriated in the Tent's casualness. The informality of dress has been legendary, with many in shorts, T-shirts and sneakers by day, sweat shirts and parkas by night, and before Aspen's more recent black tie crowd kicked in, the Tent's closest brush with formal wear may have been a black jumpsuit on which a tuxedo had been sketched. Sociologically, Tent audiences are upper income, well educated, older, roughly seventeen percent local, sixty-three percent Americans from other states and less than two percent from other countries.

The upper strata profile doesn't dampen their behavior, for they applaud a well-executed piano move and frequently applauded a chronically late violist who was mistaken for the concertmaster. By Aspen standards, a piece that fails to receive at least three curtain calls, or a concert without at least one standing ovation, can almost be pronounced a failure. Commented Misha Dichter, "We all smile a little benignly at the fact that if a piece is played loud and reasonably well, the standing ovation is automatic. Three walks out, whistles, hoots—but it's touching and shows that people appreciate it, and artists like that." Nadja Salerno-Sonnenberg had a before-and-after perspective on Aspen audiences. After she won the Naumburg Award she still played for the usual listeners, but after she was featured in a segment on *Sixty Minutes* and appeared on Johnny Carson's *Tonight Show*, she drew an additional and quite different crowd. "Suddenly I was a kind of celebrity and everywhere I went after that it was always jammed, including here. It was strange to be treated like that in Aspen.

People who've never gone to a concert come to hear me play because of the TV stuff and I think it's great—because if they had a great time, it wasn't just me, it was the symphony too. They may become subscribers, music lovers."

♪♪♪

The crowds that holler for musicians are also fans of the Tent, though serious listeners among them have had reservations from the beginning. Many musicians had difficulty hearing themselves and each other. Wind and brass were too far from the conductor and had to anticipate the beat to play in time with the strings. The conductor sometimes miscalculated the balance because acoustics at the podium differed from those in the audience. Canvas as a material neither reflects sound from the inside nor fends it from the outside, so other variables were adjusted. Baffles were angled to bolster the basses, cellos were added because basses still didn't project enough, extra strings were added to balance the brass, and the orchestra grew to gerrymander sound as well as to train students. Non-musical eruptions competed from outside. Crowds armed with small children increasingly crammed the grass on weekend afternoons, sometimes only to picnic and work on their tans, unaware that the Tent wasn't doing a band concert and that others had actually come to listen. Solo dogs diminished with the leash law but some on leashes were deaf to master's voice. Planes were instructed to avoid air space over the Tent during concerts and an infractor was actually intercepted by a concertgoer, who rushed outside with binoculars, caught the plane's number and provoked an official rebuke.

Logically there was no accounting for the fate of Laszlo Varga, whose cello performances in the seventies inherited the downpours that greeted Fernando Valenti's harpsichord pieces in the fifties and sixties. One summer he began Kodály's *Sonata for Cello Alone* under a seamless sky, only to be joined by a wailing ambulance. In the summer of 1988, years after the Varga Effect was first noticed in print, the evening concert went smoothly until just before Varga's entrance, when a deluge struck, leaving him to saw his way through one more inaudible performance. If virga is rain that evaporates before it reaches the ground, Varga was rain that struck canvas.

Musicians reacted variously to these offenses. For James Conlon the Tent was "like an eccentric aunt or the family dog." Misha Dichter stopped playing solo in the summer of 1986 "because I threw up my hands at trying to make piano music alone. I also don't like the sound of the piano with orchestra, strings or voice either, but at least you're accompanied in your unhappiness." For Zara Nelsova the problem was backstage. "The only thing I don't like is not having a comfortable place to warm up. In the little dressing rooms the sound is so live that you can't even hear yourself and there's no room to bow the instrument. I like a carpet on the floor and the right chair. If they gave me a proper dressing room, I wouldn't care what I walked out to." Lynn Harrell specifically attacked the Bayer-designed Tent. "The Saarinen tent was much better. Benches were made of pine, the resonant wood that stringed instruments are made of, and the stage was also wooden supported with beams so that it vibrated like a drum. Bayer replaced it with plywood over cement, eliminating the echo chamber. I have friends who say about Aspen, 'I hate playing there, it has such crappy acoustics.' For a Festival of this caliber, it's a disgrace."

With complaints about the Tent nearly as old as the Festival itself, many had dreamed of alternatives over the years and Gordon Hardy started to sift ideas in the late seventies. When Robert Harth became director and CEO of the Festival, he made the building of what eventually became the Joan and Irving Harris Concert Hall a priority, even over increasing faculty salaries, because he thought it would lend the Festival a needed sense of permanence. Reversing the remark trustee Courtlandt Barnes had made some thirty-five years earlier—"We just want a tent we can roll up and put in our garage"—Harth said, "We shouldn't be an organization that folds up its tent every year." Before work could begin, the Festival needed approval to build from the City of Aspen and in October 1989, the month of his arrival, Harth wrote a letter about masterplanning the Aspen Meadows in which he proposed a new "rehearsal hall." It was Gordon Hardy, in fact, who had consistently called the facility a rehearsal hall to get it through zoning over the objections of West End neighbors who feared it would generate more traffic. Harth thereafter always referred to Harris as a "rehearsal-performance hall" and points out that, in practice, five times more of its time is scheduled for rehearsing than performing, but is resigned to having entered Aspen folklore as "the guy who turned a rehearsal hall into a performance hall." After more skirmishing with West End residents the hall was approved, but there are former Planning and Zoning members who still refer to the facility, facetiously, as the Harris Rehearsal Hall, and an Aspen Ski Company official, exhausted from trying to get Forest Service approval to expand the Snowmass Ski Area onto Burnt Mountain, said, "We should have called it a rehearsal mountain."

Before it could expand, however, the Festival needed to own the land, and it didn't even own the Tent site. As part of the Aspen Institute complex, its landlords had included hoteliers and banks, none of whom ever threatened cultural activities but who retained the right to build right to the tent flap if they so chose. For years the Festival had rented from the Aspen Institute the land beneath the Tent, plus a perimeter of some ten feet around the canvas, for a dollar a year. Negotiations were protracted, with the Festival, the International Design Conference and the Aspen Center for Physics aligned as a group against the changing ownership of the Institute. It wasn't until 1991 that the Festival acquired the deed to the tent meadow. The next need was money. Senior development officer Kathy Buchanan initiated the Aspen Meadows Campaign with a goal of $12 million, of which $7 million was slated for Harris Hall, $1 million for campus renovation and the balance for the Festival's permanent endowment. Almost immediately the Aspen Foundation awarded a grant of $750,000, quickly followed by $350,000 from the National Endowment for the Arts. Joan and Irving Harris, for whom the hall was named, led the individual donors, and Colorado's four leading foundations—the Boettcher, Gates, Coors, and El Pomar Foundations—all awarded grants, as did the Kresge Foundation in Michigan. Aspen Music Festival board members kicked in an impressive $5.5 million, and with the goal reached so soon, construction of the hall began a year earlier than planned.

The time made up during fundraising was nearly lost during construction. The design, by Aspen architect Harry Teague, was complex, for the hall was to occupy an underground hollow spanned by a roof that spread like wings, with sod running up the back. Its profile would not compete with the Tent and from certain angles it would seem an extension of the surrounding meadow. The engineering was demanding, for the forty-foot deep walls needed to withstand pressure from the surrounding earth equal to the wind load on a fifty-story building the width of the hall, while the sixty-five foot roof span had to support up to 115 pounds per square foot of snow. The solution has been described as "a giant erector set filled with concrete, with flying buttresses supporting the roof."

The roof was built first so as to keep the rest dry for the pouring of concrete, and the hall was constructed "upside down and inside out." Complicating construction was the 1992–93 winter, one of the severest on record. When serious snow began in late October, the cavity was complete but concrete had just begun to be poured and only seven of the forty-six steel columns were in place. Fifty inches of snow fell during the opening eleven-day blizzard and by the ninth of June, 240 inches of snow had fallen on the construction site. Removal of snow and ice and the thawing of frozen ground preceded each construction maneuver.

Warming their hands at fires that supplemented propane and natural gas heaters, the wind howling through a shroud of Visqueen, the crews worked ten-hour days, six- and seven-day weeks. By the end of May construction was fifty days behind schedule and the City of Aspen granted a variance for construction to begin at five in the morning. After Design Conference and then the Festival began, hours when they could make noise were severely restricted. It seemed nearly miraculous that the hall was ready for its Opening Gala Concert on August 20, 1993. A few weeks before, the Emerson Quartet demonstrated the sound, designed by acoustician Elizabeth Cohen, for a select gathering of patrons. The musicians lifted their bows, began to play, no sound emerged, and there was a moment of panic. They were playing a centimeter over the strings to give everyone a jolt, and when they lowered their bows, the sound was pronounced glorious.

There was no time for landscaping, so the approach looked like the construction site it was. The façade, under the shallow folds of the roofline, was unprepossessing, being, after all, the foyer to a cavern, and the upper lobby's outer wall was a pair of commercial garage doors. Opening nighters made cracks like "Tomorrow I'm pulling up to the second bay for an oil change." A wide staircase of shallow steps led to a long, thin and high underground foyer, then through soundproof doors to the hall itself. Concertgoers emerged in a soaring expanse that widened from the stage, then tapered toward the back, a five-hundred seat auditorium completely lined in cherry and white maple of differing shapes and textures, with no parallel lines or perpendicular beams. The architect likened it to "a buried wooden instrument"—perhaps a cubist mandolin. So vivid and well-calculated are the acoustics that Harris has been called "the first concert hall of the twenty-first century." The *Denver Post* referred to Harris Hall as "the Carnegie Hall of the West," and when former Festival artistic director Ara Guzelimian became artistic advisor of Carnegie Hall in 1998, he referred to Carnegie as "the Harris Hall of the East."

Many musicians would rather play in Harris to a third of the crowd they could reach in the Tent and it provides a home for Aspen's winter concert series, which for decades had floundered between various flawed venues. Every triumph does have its critics. Snapped a lodge owner reaching daylight after a premiere concert, "I do not intend to spend my Saturday afternoons in that bunker." Said Stuart Sankey, otherwise an admirer of Harris, "It's too small, but that's the fault of the City and its zoning process. The West End homeowners have the power." Those who listened on the lawn east of the Tent were dismayed to be displaced, but when the landscaping was complete, an expanded and bermed lawn bloomed to the south and west, providing better free listening and balancing the sodded heights of Harris.

Naming Opportunities

THE ASPEN MUSIC FESTIVAL, with its hundreds of artists and students and concerts, its tent and tech crews, its tons of pianos coming and going, its annual fund drives and housing crises, its audiences in the tens of thousands, its massive complexity, suggests a battery of questions. Who gets invited? How do concert programs get selected? How much are artists paid? How is their housing determined? Who gets asked back and who gets dropped? Who has the power? How, in sum, does the whole thing work?

Curiously, over the years the process has seemed as opaque to musicians as it has to the general public. Even regular faculty have suffered the annual anxiety, as winter quickened to spring, of whether they would be invited back or whether they should make other plans for the summer. In recent years the Festival has sent a "Festival Highlights" mailing of its upcoming season during the winter, but the full program of concerts seldom appears until late May, annually convulsing those who are planning the hand-out program that has swelled to a square-bound book with hundreds of bios and program notes. Organizing two months of music instruction and performance has become a fulltime job for thirty-three employees and dozens more part timers. It is huge and, to anyone attempting to grasp it, amorphous.

The Festival has always had, to be sure, its trustees and music committees and bylaws, a mutating structure to govern its affairs. It has also been run, to a degree, by those most interested in doing so: those who offered themselves as problem solvers. In the early Hardy years, for instance, Gordon Hardy and Victor Gottlieb would get together with pieces of paper and plot the Festival. "We'll put the Julliard Quartet here, the Symphony there. ...." Gottlieb's son Larry, present at some of these sessions, recalled, "There was a sense of let's do this, let's try that. It was joyful, innocent, even childlike." The process doesn't suggest a secret plan so much as a gradual consensus reached among a nucleus of people who have, in a formal sense, no plan at all. Said Jorge Mester of his tenure, "We had an unusual and nondefinable organizational chart. It worked out very well because no one was very jealous of his own territory. Inviting people was a fluid process, a kind of consensus between Gordon Hardy, the artistic administrator, the orchestra manager, the executive vice-president and me. Sometimes we got suggestions from the Music Committee, which was advisory and elected by the musicians themselves. It was a painful process because there was no tenure here—tenure, in my opinion, is awful—but we tried to keep a sense of continuity and good fellowship." In other words, a central group whose members held positions with the Festival got together and hashed it out.

The selection of the program during Jorge Mester's tenure reduced to much the same stew. In Mester's words, "We sent out a list of things we hoped to see on the program, then solicited suggestions from the faculty. We culled from their ideas what best fit a particular summer, then had to coordinate who was here at the right time for pieces that involved more than one player." Many of the suggestions for those pieces originated with Martin Verdrager, who began studying repertoire in his early teens and had amassed a broad knowledge of what music was out there, as well as how to keep track of it for the Festival. "I was always studying scores like a conductor, just out of interest, and went to publishers to check out new music. I started keeping track of movements and opus numbers for the programs, since the number of concerts was increasing so drastically. After the first year they hired me to do it. Our calendars became models of musicological research. Other festivals wondered how we did it."

Unlike a university situation, where salaries are public knowledge, at the Festival both fees and housing have always been negotiated individually with each faculty member, remained secret, and were hence the subject of much speculation and gossip. Few faculty members were ever lured into divulging and knowledge was gained by inference. Said Zara Nelsova, "The Festival found houses for me, but I'd rather not go into the financing of it because everyone makes different arrangements. It has literal ups and downs. I loved having a house on Red Mountain, but on the other hand my students couldn't afford cabs so I had to keep ferrying them back and forth with their cellos." Kurt Oppens found the secrecy not so mysterious. "Not knowing what anybody else was getting was understandable in that it was such a jigsaw, with pieces, schedules and players to juggle, that it was simply too complicated to be clear public knowledge." Public and players alike have had to content themselves that an inner group, with the welfare of the Festival at heart, benignly worked it out.

On the eve of the fiftieth anniversary season, Robert Harth elaborated the current system. Each faculty member is evaluated annually at contract time, factoring in the individual's amount of teaching and playing, number of students, years of service and relative standing among others who play the same instrument. There isn't much need for new faculty because of a strong core, but if absence or resignation creates an opening for, say a bassoonist, "We call Music Director David Zinman and get his opinion, then we call the bassoon faculty and say, 'Here are the ones David likes—do we have connections?' The music director knows how the bassoonists play and the faculty knows how they teach. We compare the two lists and see where they intersect. The choosing of faculty, guest artists and conductors involves the music director, the artistic administration department, the general manager, myself, and the dean of students. The dean looks at guest artists as potential teachers of master classes. I like it to be interactive, with different points of view—and the final decision is the music director's."

The selection process for repertoire has been modified, and in the case of chamber works the choices now emanate primarily from the players themselves. When chamber music was assigned, with staff putting players together, artists sometimes wound up not liking the pieces or their fellow players. Under the revised system, during the fall all chamber players receive a request form on which they list the pieces they would like to play, with which colleagues. Usually they confer among themselves before they fill out the forms, then submit more than they will wind up playing, increasing the odds of liking the result. The staff goes through it, trying to accommodate the musicians as much as possible while balancing the programs. Says Harth, "When faculty are displeased we try to honor them next year, but the science is imperfect."

The choice of orchestral repertoire puts the needs of students foremost. Many may be aiming for solo careers and may even chafe at so much orchestral playing, but Harth has seen an increasing competitiveness within the last twenty years. With so many talented graduates entering a limited job market, many know they will wind up in orchestras and they want to learn repertoire that will serve future employment, including that crucial step, the orchestral audition. "A lot of obscure repertoire isn't necessarily in their best interest," says Harth. "Contemporary repertoire is important so that they know the styles, including being able to read contemporary scores, but a lot of kids haven't even played the standards yet. What appeals to students for professional reasons also appeals to a mainstream audience. That's important because if students play to an empty house, it destroys morale and for the Festival it affects donations and ticket sales. We are still far more adventuresome than other festivals and our audiences are open-minded, but we have to balance esoteric repertoire with what audiences and students want."

Misha Dichter reinforces Harth's argument for the standards by describing performances of the Tchaikowsky Piano Concerto he played the same week in Philadelphia and in Aspen. "Needless to say the Philadelphia played it better because they've played it five zillion times, but there wasn't the look of discovery on the faces of the players that you have here, with our mix of professionals and students. Larry Foster rehearsed it as if it were a world premiere, while in Philadelphia they'd look at their watches and say, we've played this piece before, don't bother us."

Choosing repertoire demands further considerations. Explains Harth, "Will there be enough playing for low brass? Is it so weighted for strings that the trombones have nothing to do? Instrumentalists who don't have enough to play aren't having the summer they expected, so repertoire choice includes instrumentation. Also, we have to look at the programs as wholes. The general manager needs to gauge it from a production standpoint— the rehearsal times, stage changes, the feasibility of the works themselves. We can't program two works in a row in the same key, or schedule too much tough playing in one concert. And we have to program more difficult works later in the season, when the orchestras are more seasoned." It is a staggering list of demands—so complex that no one has figured a way to computerize the variables and the Festival has had to fall back on the human mind.

The student application process has come a long way from the early days of the Festival when pupils, invited by their teachers or simply following them, were virtually self-selected. In those days there were few summer festivals and still fewer that offered instruction. The popularity of summer music has swelled until there are festivals in every state—incredibly, twelve in Colorado alone. Festivals compete for the same pool of students, so that from the student standpoint the selection of a summer program is a form of comparative shopping.

For Aspen the process begins in the fall, when a recruiter tours universities and conservatories to make presentations, hand out catalogues and answer questions. Mailed-in applications include the first three choices of teachers and a tape with required pieces. Faculty members read the applications, listen to the tapes and accept more than they will wind up teaching, for some will choose to go elsewhere. Economically, there are three categories of students: full-paying, scholarships and fellowships. Before financial aid, tuition for all students is the same: in 1999 it was $2,150. Those who receive scholarship money must audition live before faculty members who make themselves available at ten locations around the country. Scholarships involve financial help and full scholarship includes tuition, room, board and a stipend of two thousand dollars for the summer. There are 160 full scholarships, which run the gamut from instrument playing to conducting to opera; they are renewable for three years and require live auditions. This mixed student body has twice topped one thousand— in 1989 and 1995—but has been progressively cut back, with an ultimate goal of 850 students. According to Harth, reducing the number of students improves the student-faculty ratio, with more attention for each student and less strain on each teacher, and the school can be more selective in its admissions. Below 850, believes Harth, the quantity of students wouldn't achieve the critical mass that allows the school to work both musically and economically.

The primacy of students is reflected in the Festival's economics. The average American symphony orchestra receives forty-five to fifty-five percent of its funding from ticket sales. In Aspen that figure is a mere seventeen percent, while twenty-five percent derives from student tuitions—with the rest made up by grants, individual donations and assorted forms of fundraising and earned income. In the absence of the kind of large cash-ladling endowment that every arts organization aspires to, the annual fundraising drive has kept the Festival solvent. Throughout the summer the Festival presents benefit concerts—Tent-packing sessions by the Festival's own Jazz Ensemble as well as five decades of guest appearances that have included Duke Ellington, Victor Borge, Ravi Shankar, Dudley Moore, John Denver, Jack Benny, George Shearing, Garrison Keillor, Michael Feinstein, Danny Kaye, and Anna Russell narrating the complete plot of Wagner's *Ring* to the convulsed.

Two further moneymakers are institutions that stand to either side of the entrance to the Tent. The lemonade stand, founded by trustee Bob Marsh and operated by a succession of faculty offspring and Aspen volunteers, is less known for lemonade than for coffee and homemade cookies consumed amid swirls of gossip, with proceeds going to the Fred O. Lane Memorial Scholarship Fund. The idea for the Gift Kiosk began in 1979 when a young man, fueled by a case of beer, peddled T-shirts at the entrance to the Tent and donated the proceeds to the Festival. Trustee Jan Collins saw a promising idea and suggested to Festival junkie Gairt Mauerhoff that he open an official stand, and since 1980 the Kiosk, founded by Mauerhoff, has been selling Festibilia that include T-shirts, posters, pins, keyboard-motif watches and scarfs, select books and annual surprises that help support the Aspen Music School Scholarship Fund. In Aspen as elsewhere, inventiveness and patchwork keep the arts out of the red.

After the arrival of some fifteen hundred musicians nearly on the same day in June, the Festival endures a day of registration, followed by two days of auditions for orchestra assignments. The process is particularly cumbersome for string players. Around 150 show up at once and another thirty arrive late. During registration they are given one of two pieces to prepare, the more difficult for students over fifteen. Over the next two days, two or three faculty members listen to them play the prepared piece, part of a concerto of their own choosing and a surprise piece to sight-read, enough of a spectrum to reveal technical abilities and levels of sophistication. Some students prefer the big-piece repertoire of the Festival Orchestra, others the more exposed playing of the Chamber Symphony, and those choices—or preferences for the three other orchestras—are honored if the playing qualifies. Stand partners are balanced so that a technically strong player may be matched with a more musical player with less facility. Except for a core group at the front of a section, the stands are rotated so no one gets stuck near the back: in the Festival Orchestra, for instance, typically four stands are permanent and six shift positions. The judges make notes on all they can so that if students later want to change orchestras, the faculty will have baseline data on advisability, and the Festival Orchestra is large enough that if a student wants to take a week off to focus on practicing, a substitute is easily found. Because there is a partial turnover of students mid-season, the audition process must be repeated for another fifty students later in the summer. Balancing so many wishes and abilities is laborious, but there are no shortcuts if students are to be treated as individuals.

Along with the varied instrumental instruction there are smaller programs little known to the public. There is, for instance, the Center for Advanced Quartet Studies, in which student quartets train intensively with such established quartets as the American, the Emerson and the Orion. There is an annual symposium on the medical problems of musicians, which treats the occupational hazards of bending over cellos, risking tendinitis through repetitive movement or coping with stage fright. There are the composition programs, the conducting fellowships, the piano tuning apprenticeships, the audio recording institute and the opera program. The Aspen Opera Theater Center, under the direction of

Edward Berkeley, offers classes in acting, diction, body movement, relaxation, and scene and role preparation, not to mention singing. Continuing the tradition initiated by Madeleine Milhaud back in the fifties, the Opera Theater offers three productions every summer, including traditional favorites by Mozart, Verdi and Puccini along with such contemporary works as Augusta Read Thomas' *Lygeia*, based on a tale by Edgar Allen Poe; William Turnage's *Greek*, an updating of Sophocles' *Oedipus* set in contemporary London; and Thomas Ades' *Powder Her Face*, in which the scandalous doings of the Duchess of Argyll are sung and enacted on stage. Particularly popular with the public are Saturday morning master classes in which scenes from various operas are performed with an eye toward making them theatrically as well as musically convincing.

The Festival has managed to turn even the recording of itself into a teaching opportunity. Concerts were first recorded in 1958 when trustee Edgar Stanton suspended a microphone over the Tent stage and captured what he could. Gairt Mauerhoff, who turned his attention from the Gift Kiosk to the recording program in 1990, has been transferring those early tapes onto compact disks to preserve them. He finds that their quality and selection vary wildly from year to year, indicating that at first Stanton recorded only his personal favorites or that he threw away the technical failures. Some tapes are only partial concerts and others are over-recorded, perhaps because the mike was too close to the musicians and distorted the sound. During one period the tapes were manufactured from a material that has since stuck together, requiring the reels to be baked at a low temperature for half an hour to separate them. However primitive they may sound now, the Stanton tapes were broadcast for years over Voice of America, so that Aspen concerts during the Cold War extended their reach behind the Iron Curtain.

Recording is more sophisticated at the Edgar Stanton Audio Recording Studio, endowed in 1990 by Stanton's widow, Rose

Stanton. Two or three state-of-the-art mikes are used for each concert, manipulated by an engineer assisted by interns and students. Each summer six or more audio students arrive for an intensive four-week session that includes a workshop, hands-on experience of recording concerts, and guest lectures from wellknown audio engineers. All concerts, including student recitals and many master classes, are now recorded for the permanent Festival archive.

As the recordings are finished, and after the Festival, Gairt Mauerhoff transfers them to tapes that are sold to performers, students, faculty and staff. Before he took over, says Mauerhoff, the dubbing, or transcription of tapes, was mostly done by students working after midnight—"kids spinning dials"—but now the tapes are edited to eliminate audience noise and long pauses for tuning between movements. There is no eliminating the final applause, however, for Aspen audiences usually begin before the final bar and artists insist on hearing the ovation for their piece, however much it may resemble static to the nonperformer. Composition students are the most eager to get their tapes immediately. For copyright reasons the recordings are not available to the general public, but to musicians they are objects of study as well as vanity.

Spicing the instruction tucked into every aspect of the Festival are twelve concerto contests held throughout the summer. There are two contests each for piano and violin, involving different pieces and held early and late in the season, and wind and brass players are judged together—reflecting the number of students of respective instruments. Teachers decide which of their students should enter, with six to twelve players typically competing in a given contest, and winners cannot compete again. The jury panel is composed of faculty, including the eventual conductor of the concerto, who gains from following the winner through the process. Ever since a jury split on a winner, requiring the Franck *Variations for Piano and Orchestra* to be played twice on the same program, panels have been composed of an odd number of judges. These regularly scheduled events, numerous as they are, still don't suggest the range of student experience, for the Festival is also a laboratory for works in progress. In 1998, for instance, the youngest student orchestra, under the direction of David Zinman, with soloists and chorus from the opera department, did a reading from *The Great Gatsby*, an opera commissioned by the Metropolitan Opera of New York from John Harbison for a premiere on January 1, 2000. The Met sent five key staff persons to listen. It would have cost the composer fifty thousand dollars to hire a professional orchestra for this run-through. Instead, it became an opportunity for young students to participate in the preparation of a highly anticipated work.

Besides its self-involvement, the Festival has an ample outreach program. As early as the fifties Forestt Miller was driving students to Buena Vista and Meeker to perform concerts as part of the Young Artists of Aspen program, and Jeanne Jaffee, in her tenure as trustee, was instrumental in dispatching players to such towns as Salida, Craig and Silt, believing that it was important to gain support for the Festival on the Western Slope. The Festival began to get nervous, however, about sending students out on the road or in small planes over the mountains and in 1983 the outreach program was made an official, and thus more tightly controlled, part of the Festival.

Forrestt Miller's student concerts were always free and much of the playing within the Roaring Fork Valley is still given away. There are, for instance, three annual concerts at a park in Basalt, where families can picnic and take children too young to be allowed into the Tent. In Aspen there are Peanut Butter and Jam Sessions for two- to five-year-olds. In the Tent there is an annual family concert at which students line the inside of the canvas, explain their instruments and let members of the public play them, with food provided at an outside party tent by a sponsor. There is also an annual free concert in the courtyard of the

Aspen Valley Hospital, which diffuses music through the surrounding rooms. Deborah Barnekow, the Festival's first fulltime outreach coordinator, said of one such event, "A woman was there for chemotherapy, in great pain, and her therapist said, 'Listen to the music and see if it doesn't make you feel better.' Her nausea went away for a time, she enjoyed the concert, and when the kids heard that, they were pleased and couldn't wait to go back. It touched something in them."

Barnekow does not believe, however, that all music should be given away. She notes that students don't have the time to play on the mall anymore, particularly when they might make only ten dollars for four hours of playing, and she sees that they are reimbursed by contract when members of the public call the Festival for musicians to play at parties and weddings. The most enjoyable fundraising events are surely the concerts played to small groups in private homes such as software mogul Gideon Gartner's. On an afternoon in August 1998, for instance, fifty opera lovers who had paid forty dollars apiece heard a selection of song in Gartner's soaring livingroom, ending with the love duet that concludes Act I of *La Bohème*. In the Puccini original the lovers walk arm in arm offstage and sing the last phrase obscured by the wings, but at Gartner's they walked upstairs to the balcony and sang the phrase to the view, seen as well as heard. Proceeds from the concert went to the Aspen Opera Theater Center, and Gartner, demonstrating his own priorities, chose to be in Aspen that day rather than in New York, where a business he had built up for years was being sold.

The outreach program doesn't end when the Festival disbands in August, but operates all year, particularly in the schools. It is not just a matter of musicians showing up to play concerts, which Barnekow dismisses as "drive-by kiddie gigs," but of three two-week residencies during which music students hold classes, workshops, master classes and after-school events that give local students a more rounded experience. In 1988 the musical school year concluded with choirs from schools throughout the Roaring Fork Valley combining their voices in a single grand concert.

Finally, the kind of music the Festival brought in has escaped the Festival itself. By the beginning of the nineties, summer musicians who had moved to the Aspen area fulltime, joined by others who settled in the Roaring Fork Valley because they found it congenial, were numerous enough to provide year-around indigenous chamber music. Playing in Crested Butte, Crawford, Grand Junction and most of all in the valley itself, a changing group that includes several pianists, a violinist, a violist, an oboist, a cellist, a bassoonist and various singers performs for church services, medical conventions, memorial services, numerous weddings and the odd handbag fashion show. They are subject to vicissitudes unknown in the Tent, such as having to wait for their coats at one of Aspen's pricier homes because the coat rack tipped over from the weight of the sables, confusing everyone's wraps. They also find that Aspen, ironically, is the worst venue in terms of attendance, largely because Aspen reporters are so fixated on rock and roll that they won't cover classical music once the Tent has folded for the season. On the other hand, the local churches are particularly keen on classical music and the revolving group manages to turn out concerts featuring Bach, Brahms, Britten and the other B's—achieving the democracy of good music that is one of the classical passion's goals.

During his tenure as president Robert Harth has put his own stamp on the Festival. An early move was to close the New York office, eliminating the several weeks of time lost in the annual move and consolidating the artistic planning, which had been headquartered in New York since the early fifties, with the financial and publicity departments in Aspen. To mend fences he called the board members who had resigned in protest of Gordon Hardy, invited as many as he could rally to a meeting of the current board and made twelve of them Lifetime Trustees. Harth also returned to the shorter conductorships that marked the early years of the Festival. Lawrence Foster had taken over from Jorge Mester a year after Harth's arrival, served for six seasons and was replaced by David Zinman, conductor of the Baltimore Symphony Orchestra. From Zinman's standpoint, it was a long desired chance to work with young musicians, and a year after taking the post he resigned from Baltimore to devote himself to Aspen and to guest conducting.

In another return to earlier Festival customs Harth reinstated the Monday-off policy, encouraging students to take a break from practicing. There was no bringing back the all-Festival Monday picnics, or canceling evening rehearsals, let alone Monday night chamber concerts. Most students at first still used even Monday daylight to work on their chops, but a Thursday newsletter, *Soundings*, introduced in 1996, began publishing details of upcoming horseback rides, rafting trips and Gondola rides, and Music School Dean Hal Laster leads Monday morning hikes that are particularly appealing to city kids who hesitate to strike out on their own. Gradually students have been discovering that a rounded life is possible, even at Music School.

After a several-year rest in the wake of the Harris Hall campaign—necessary to fundraisers as well as donors—the Future in Concert campaign was launched with numerous goals, one of which was to solve, forever, the annual crisis in housing. The problem was as old as the Festival itself and those with long memories could lament, with Herta Glaz, "After the second year, when we said goodbye to Mr. Paepcke, he said, 'I'm making you an offer. I am willing to sell each of you as many acres as you want for fifty dollars an acre.' We thought he just wanted to get rid of property because things weren't working. Of course at that time there was no electricity, no water, and you thought, what would I do with an acre of nothing?" A few faculty members did gain their own housing when Fritz Benedict created the Aspen Grove subdivision and begged musicians to buy. Szymon Goldberg accepted a free piece of land, and Adele Addison and

Brooks Smith built houses. A few other musicians, far-sighted or lucky, bought Aspen property in the fifties and sixties, but that was little help to a Festival that ultimately needed to bed some fifteen hundred people each summer.

Aggravating the problem was that a town once laced with shacks and miners' cabins became swollen with condominiums and cavernous but vacant second homes, while the land base remained narrow and fixed. Locals who once rented to musicians for a pittance eventually cashed in on visitors, or simply died out. The Tiptons lost the housing they had enjoyed for twelve years because the house's new owners would be in Aspen for the summer; the newcomers came for a week and the rest of the season the house stood empty. Charles Jones had been a regular at the Festival for thirty-eight years, spending thirty years in one house and seven in another, and in 1988 he was stashed in a small apartment without a piano. That same year, one hundred students, otherwise accepted, were unable to attend the Festival because rents were too high, and smaller low-cost lodges that accommodated students were one by one closing shop. A few enterprising students already familiar with Aspen have been able to line up their own housing, and fellowship students can have a housing or a living stipend—but the stipends haven't been able to keep up with the market.

The affluent new Aspen, spectacular source of fundraising, was also spectacularly out of touch. One well-intentioned organization even decided it could inspire inner city black youngsters by giving them a tour of Starwood, Aspen's most exclusive gated community, with black faculty members and students serving as guides and role models. Vocal teacher George Shirley and his student Tiffany Jackson were enlisted. As he exclaimed in disbelief, "The guard house *alone* ... Tiffany came from a tough neighborhood in Bridgeport, Connecticut, and was level-headed enough to assess the place, though even to her it was unreal. But what about kids from the ghetto? If they do aspire to Starwood, how do they get there—by working with discipline or by selling drugs?" Cost and living space rather than culture shock may have been at the heart of the Festival housing problem, but untenanted ostentation, along with soaring rents, had so displaced the ability to put people up that plans were floated to move the Festival to Snowmass or even Durango.

The first real breakthrough was the Marolt Ranch Dormitory, with room for three hundred students, built at the south end of city-owned Marolt Park in 1991. Conveniently set between Aspen and the music campus, the complex included a dining room with indoor and outdoor seating to replace the student eateries that had been installed over the years in such venues as the basement of the Wheeler Opera House and the Aspen Valley Hospital, and the plan was so successful that architect Harry Teague was soon afterward chosen to design Harris Hall. Another two hundred students have since been accommodated in dormitories on land the Festival acquired with Future in Concert funds at the Burlingame Ranch, near the Aspen airport.

Housing was only a small part of the ambitious Future in Concert campaign, whose goal was no less than thirty-two million dollars. The major portion of these funds, eighteen million dollars, has been dedicated to the endowment the Festival has long needed, with up to five percent, or nine hundred thousand dollars, to be spent annually and the rest reinvested to build up the fund. Roughly a third of that annual expenditure fortifies the salaries, housing and transportation of faculty and guest artists; another third goes toward scholarships and other forms of student assistance; and the balance is divided between such items as building maintenance, archives and program development. The best news is that students who are talented but strapped need no longer be turned away, and Judy Hancock, Director of Development and coordinator of the campaign, has made the underappreciated point that out-of-towners have a stake in the welfare of Aspen students, for many are the future musicians of their own home towns.

The Future in Concert's other fourteen million dollars was dedicated toward capital improvements such as the new housing at the Burlingame Ranch, much needed improvements at the music campus, from better insulation for practice rooms that are often freezing to compliance with the Americans with Disabilities Act, and what the Festival's glossy brochure for the Future in Concert campaign spoke of as "enriched acoustics, new audience amenities, and improved sightlines ... in the Bayer-Benedict Tent."

Sometime after the Future in Concert Campaign was made public, the Festival exploded its political bombshell—that the Bayer-designed canvas tent was in fact to be replaced with a permanent structure designed by Harry Teague. Such a move had been contemplated since Herbert Bayer's abortive proposal to encase the Festival in cinderblocks in 1964, but this was the first literally solid proposal since. Alarm, wild with rumor, was instantaneous among the canvas tent's defenders. An elaborate scale model of the proposal was displayed in the lobby of Harris Hall, then in front of the Bayer Tent itself, to be scrutinized and critiqued by all. Over the years, what Firkušný in his Czech accent had called "that tent of bias"—meaning "that tent of Bayer's"— had become Aspen's signature structure, arguably more sacred to its citizens than any of its churches. Any proposal to replace it had to pass Planning and Zoning and Aspen City Council, ensuring voluble debate. Some argued that memories of the town, high school graduations as well as concerts, were bound up in the existing tent and we would be losing our common heritage. Robert Harth's having referred to Harris Hall as a rehearsal hall was itself rehearsed in the papers, with the implication that the Festival didn't always level with the public. When the project came up for a vote at City Council, Lynn Harrell, who had sedulously avoided participation in Aspen politics until then, made a passionate plea in its favor. After the months of politicking, editorials and letters to the editor, no one could claim that final approval had been pulled off in secret.

Teague's design, in fact, was an inventive blend of tradition and the needs of a better facility. The structure kept the height and footprint of the existing tent, but lowered the interior eight feet to accommodate 250 more people and buffer the sound from the outside. The shape was octagonal, with four lean steel columns supporting a circular shell of white Teflon-coated fiberglass, so that both shape and material simulated the look of the existing tent while the Teflon mix reflected sound rather than blotting it like mildewing canvas. A "vertical louver closure system"—in demotic, sets of pivoting upright slats controlled by horizontal bars—adjusted the passage of light, ventilation and sound between the interior and the lawn seating area. The stage was tiered, with permanent risers for choral groups behind the orchestra. Elevators conducted the disabled between ground and stage levels and a tunnel to Harris Hall allowed instruments—crucially, pianos—to commute between the two venues. Backstage there was new storage space, along with a Green Room and dressing rooms that would please even Zara Nelsova. The sides of the structure would still be open to the mountains, retaining the sense of a tent out in the sagebrush. Still available for the International Design Conference of Aspen and high school graduations, the new facility would be used only during the summer season and winter concerts would remain in Harris Hall.

The summer of 1999, the fiftieth anniversary of the Goethe Bicentennial, was celebrated as the fiftieth summer of the Aspen Music Festival, though sticklers held that the first year when music was an actual festival, rather than the adjunct to a conference, was 1950. Gordon and Lilian Hardy were proclaimed honorary chairmen and Steinway made fifty commemorative Aspen pianos with marquetry aspen branch-and-leaf designs on the legs and music racks—only the fourth limited edition piano in Steinway's 147-year history. The programming extravaganza featured the return of James Levine, after a twenty-six-year absence, to conduct a Chamber Symphony program that included the *Ricer-*

care from Bach's "Musical Offering" in an unusual transcription by Anton Webern, along with Mahler's Symphony No. 3 with the Festival Orchestra.

It was a year of cycles: the Emerson String Quartet played the first five Shostakovich quartets, Lynn Harrell performed all six Bach suites for cello and Yefim Bronfman played the five Beethoven concertos. Ticketless piano fans awaited Vladimir Feltsman's last-minute permission to sit onstage for his sold-out program of Bach and Mussorgsky. Besides the usual three operas in the Wheeler Opera House, opera buffs were treated to concert performances of Alban Berg's *Wozzeck*, Wagner's *Göt-terdämmerung*, Act III and, for a grand finale, Verdi's *Aida* in its entirety: an opera commissioned for the opening of the Suez Canal also rang down the Tent. On a quieter note, Lynn Harrell presented a program called "Songs My Father Taught Me" devoted to Mack Harrell, who had sung at the Goethe Bicentennial and during the early years of the Festival; a deeply moved audience heard recordings of Mack Harrell singing, followed by his son Lynn playing his father's favorite music on the cello. Levine made his first public appearance by slipping unexpectedly into the Tent while Lynn Harrell was rehearsing Richard Strauss' *Don Quixote*, provoking Harrell to mug Quixote's reactions to the orchestra for Levine's benefit.

Fundraising for the new tent reached fever pitch, with sequential signs along a footpath from the parking tent spouting "Our new tent must/Be paid for soon/Your timely gift/Keeps us in tune" and other attempts at Burma Shavian wit, while the usual movie posters under glass by the Gift Kiosk were replaced by updates on the fundraising campaign. At the entrance to the Tent, next to the scale model of the Teague Tent, stood Noël Congdon, Chair of the Board of Trustees, extolling it with zeal to all who passed, and before each Sunday afternoon concert a fundraising plea was delivered by Congdon, tent task force chair Joan Harris, violinist Robert McDuffie and other notables. The weather pitched in with monsoons that drove rain into canvas punctually at concert time, drowning out pieces, causing music to be repeated, and giving stopped conductors an opportunity to lecture the audience on the need for a new facility. When the rain honored Gordon Hardy by leaking through the canvas drop by drop on his head, he discreetly wiped it off with a handkerchief, but after rain splattered a Steinway during a Beethoven piano concerto, Bronfman made a proper show of wiping it dry between movements.

Partisans of the old canvas, meanwhile, sentimentally relished experiences of the flaws of yesteryear. One night Jimmy Lin had to stop playing because of mysterious fortissimo screeching. He left the stage, then returned to inform the audience, "Two raccoons are getting it on backstage." The penultimate Chamber Symphony concert took place one day after the last solar eclipse of the century, a swath of momentary blackouts across Europe from England to Turkey. Those on the west side of the Tent watched a ray of sun harpoon a round-faced, silver-haired gentleman, elevating him from the dark audience. Suddenly a shadow the same size as his head flickered back and forth across his face, its own features superimposed in Picasso-like profile upon the radiant frontal portrait. The sun, conductor Nicholas McGegan and listener were in perfect alignment, creating flickering eclipses of the listener, and on a couple of occasions the conductor paused so that his head fully covered that of the round-faced concert-goer who, even more briefly than Romania the previous day, achieved totality. When the movement of Haydn was over, the conductor, so lightstruck in his left eye that he could barely focus the score, signaled a tent crew member to tighten a sagging canvas panel—an adjustment that would be accomplished merely by pulling a bar of the vertical louver closure system once the new tent was up.

Another odd strand of that memorable season was such a passion for naming features of the Festival that someone dubbed it Appellation Summer. It was decided, for instance, that Fritz Benedict's name would remain on the new tent designed by Harry Teague. The Bayer-designed tent had originally been just the Bayer Tent, but when Fritz Benedict made a land trade that allowed for construction of the Marolt Dormitory, the Festival chose to honor him by adding his name to the Tent. The revised name, the Bayer-Benedict Tent, was doubly ironic in that Bayer dissociated himself from the Tent as soon as the musicians changed the shape of the stage and Benedict didn't want his name on it because, as an architect, he had not participated in its design. Now deceased, he had no part in the Teague Tent either, but it became the Benedict Music Tent because the Festival wished to perpetuate his honor by affixing his name to the Tent, though this time the late Herbert Bayer was off the hook. But nomenclature had far more than a tent to cope with. Future concertgoers would enter a Music Festival Park bearing a donor's name, cross a named Court and a named Terrace appointed with named Benches, enter a named Entrance, descend a named Stairway to occupy one of the named Seats that face the named Stage with its named Chorus Risers and named Podium, assured that musicians backstage were enjoying their named Dressing Rooms and named Green Room. Attendees would be spared, however, from sipping from the Betty Russell Drinking Fountain, for years ago the plaque had slipped off and the fountain had reverted to anonymity. The naming opportunities, however immoderate, paid off, for it was the Festival's financial footing that had heretofore existed in name only.

Hearing the Sun

ONE OF THE FIFTY-YEAR traditions of this festival pitched in a mining town gone to seed has been its playfulness, its humorous camaraderie. For years, for instance, a group of musicians ran from town to Dudley's Diner, a restaurant in the Aspen Airport Business Center, to eat *huevos rancheros*, a tradition started by Robert McDuffie. The first year they ran, ate *huevos*, ran back and were sick the rest of the day; thereafter the group enlisted supporters to meet them in cars for the ride home, allowing Lawrence Dutton, Misha Dichter, Stephen Clapp and crowd to extend the run to the Rio Grande Trail, over the bridge behind the water purification plant and up the hill to food. In 1990 reservations were made for twenty, though only seven made the run, and on one occasion violinist Mark Peskanov arrived at Dudley's by taxi in his jogging shorts and a suit jacket, smoking a cigarette. In the same spirit, Mark Peskanov, Fred Zlotkin and Misha Dichter played Beethoven's *Ghost* Trio the year the movie *Ghostbusters* was popular; when they returned for their bows, they had torn off their coats to reveal *Ghostbuster* T-shirts Dichter had made. Commented Dichter, "You can't do that at most festivals." Comedy merged with tribute during Jorge Mester's farewell year, when Martin Verdrager took a photograph of Mester to a printer and had Mester masks, held on sticks, made en masse. When Mester arrived at the season's first after-concert reception, he was greeted by a hundred black-and-white versions of himself—the two-year-old daughter riding on his shoulders kept pointing and repeating, "Two daddy, two daddy," that being the highest number to which she could count—and Mester masks reappeared through the 1990 season.

Teasing and practical jokes have been chronic at the Festival. Zara Nelsova loved to bait the gullible and once told pianist Lee Luvisi that she would be wearing a wig during their performance, but that sometimes it got caught in the pegs when she was tuning her cello, came off and hung around her neck: if that happened, would he please get up from the piano and replace it on her head? "Oh no, I couldn't do that," said Luvisi, genuinely alarmed. Martin Verdrager engaged his friends in perpetual water wars that escalated from squirt guns to hoses and pails. In 1977, when a woman from the National Endowment for the Arts arrived to see how the grant was being spent, Assistant Dean Bill Vickery and Verdrager wined and dined her at Verdrager's apartment, extolled the Festival and then, by prearrangement, pretended to disagree on how much students should perform, escalated the mutual abuse and at last pulled out black water pistols and shot each other. Two weeks later they received a package that contained the largest automatic water gun on the market, affixed with a sticker that said, "This water gun provided by the National Endowment for the Arts." Verdrager later got his comeuppance at an elegant dinner party given by an important donor. Jorge Mester seated himself opposite Verdrager and just as the meal was about to end, Mester shot him an under-the-table drenching such that he didn't dare get up when it was time to leave.

The ultimate caper may have been pulled by a tent manager seeking revenge on his crew for jokes played on him. He bought a forty dollar violin from a Denver pawnshop, removed almost all the wood that held it together and slipped it to a complicit Robert

McDuffie after a rehearsal. McDuffie deliberately bumped into a couple of tent crew members, dropped the violin, which shattered to bits, and screamed, "My Stradivarius!"—nearly provoking heart attacks in his victims. If such joking sounds aggressive, the flip side is the sense of extended family that impelled Lynn Harrell, who was operated on in 1998 in London for carpal tunnel syndrome, to come to Aspen for his rehabilitation. Even though he was unable to play, the Festival gave him a house to stay in and made him feel he was recovering at home. "If I had to weather a career-threatening operation," he said, "the place I wanted to be was here."

Pranks and strokes of grace aren't confined to human behavior; the elements too conspire. Just as the temple was torn during a performance of Bach's *St. Matthew Passion*, a bolt of lightning lit up the sky. During Samuel Barber's *Capricorn Concerto*, the first piece performed for the 1995 season, the squawky second movement for flute, oboe and trumpet had just begun when a magpie, screeching as if it were reading its part in the score, stuck its head through an opening near the apex of the Tent and pulled at a loose piece of rope, apparently trying to free it for its nest. During a long English horn solo at a Sunday morning rehearsal of Sallinen's Symphony No. 6, bells from the Episcopalian church blended perfectly into the eerie effects. At another Sunday rehearsal, the slow movement of a Dohnányi piece ended in chimes that continued when the movement was over— the bells struck again. Mahler's *Resurrection* Symphony was to close the "Music and Nature" summer of 1996, which had begun with a mudslide, and the concert was also Lawrence Foster's farewell performance as music director. A Tent-shaking thunderstorm accompanied the tempestuous first movement and the power went out. Musicians waited, then resumed lest they lose light for reading the score, and suddenly the power returned to illuminate the Tent—mirroring the symphony's own movement from spiritual darkness to redemption. Over three decades before, on a day of grey weather, woodwinds in falling thirds had begun Ravel's *Introduction and Allegro*. When Marcella DeCray's harp swept in with a jubilant arpeggio the Tent flooded with gold, as if one could see the sound of exulting strings—or hear the sun.

As for the musical experience itself from the standpoint of a player, Carole Cowan, who has spent twenty-six summers in Aspen and is assistant concertmaster of the Festival Orchestra, sums it up. "I have the best seat in the house. Today I was playing just inches from Sarah Chang as she performed her concerto. She bumped into our stand and sprang away when she realized how close she was. Just being so close to someone so intensely involved is incredible and the energy reminded me of a time Maureen Forrester was singing a foot from me and I practically quit playing because I felt myself within her aura. Every hair on her head was vibrating and I could hardly move, it was so powerful. I told her later and she just laughed and thought it was funny. But the artists here are unbelievable. I can't think of any other place I could have played all this repertoire, such a variety of orchestral and chamber music, as well as hearing everyone else's concerts. It's been such a privilege."

♪♪ ♪

For Festival-going locals the last day of the season has always been suffused with sadness, the realization of how quickly the music has passed and the long winter to face before it happens again. After the last concert they distract themselves with parties on the grass outside the Tent, rites in which wine is prominent. A couple of weeks later, singly or in small groups, a few have watched the tent crew unlacing the canvas panels, freeing them at the top, sliding their suspending hooks down the cables, lowering them to the ground, folding them, stuffing them into canvas bags and storing them backstage as the Tent, like some hibernating animal, withdrew inside itself for the winter. Jimmy Lin once touched back after the season and described his exhilaration at seeing the Tent without its top. "As usual I walked through the back door and onto the stage, and there were the mountains! I'd never seen mountains from the stage and I was so excited that I wanted to scream and yell. I thought sometime we should play a concert without the canvas." A more local view was summarized by an Aspenite's Christmas card. The exterior, labeled "Joyeux," showed a snapshot of musicians and Aspenites celebrating at a birthday party. Inside was a photo of the sender sitting under a grey sky in the empty cement bowl, bundled up, alone, surrounded by snow. Under it was the caption, "Noël."

A quite different scene greeted the Festival buff after the last performance to play in the canvas, the blockbuster concert version of *Aida*. The light-leaking side panels were removed first, leaving the spreading white big top perched on its poles like an enormous sun hat. A workman spent the morning shoving a crowbar under the metal bench supports, uprooting them from the cement, then tipping the benches on their backs. A support crew, joshing in Spanish, carried the benches through the back of the Tent to a high heap in the Paepcke Auditorium parking lot. The torn-out bench supports left a radiating grid of pockmarks composed of crumbled cement and trapped cottonwood seed. Bench pads, blue and orange, were stacked into a partial wall where a side panel had been. Onstage, the metal risers where the chorus had sung were being dismembered with great clatter. Even as essentials were disappearing, four planters with foliage that had adorned the podium for *Aida* sent their greenery into the air like weeds in a vacant lot. The clanging of metal from all this undoing resounded so ear-piercingly that it was hard to believe that the Tent was being replaced because of bad acoustics.

Backstage, folding chairs, stools and music stands stood in isolated clumps. In the farthest room, like a survivor from Versailles, stood a golden spindly-legged Empire-style harpsichord under a royal blue protective cloth. Two crew members wheeled in an elongated dolly that fit precisely under the instruments, turned cranks, jacked it up as if it were about to receive an oil change and pushed it to a truck whose dimensions seemed calibrated to carry harpsichords. In the next room a pair of gleaming brass kettledrums, alone and bereft of their stands, leaned against each other.

The dismantling of the Tent heightened the randomness that had always characterized it. It was the belief of John Cage, inventor of the musical happening, that music was the perception of notes plus everything else going on at the same time. A rendition of Schubert, for instance, might consist of four movements, a man to your right thumbing his program, a shaft of patchouli from behind, a sunburned hiker snapping awake, an itch on your shoulderblade, four fiddlers bobbing like weeds in the wind, the shriek of magpies, scuffling, wheezing, squirming and indecipherable shivers of air. Schubert survived all this, charged with concentric rings of association. Through a retreating prospect of summers it had become difficult to separate the Festival from the musk of canvas, the stitching of light, the bite of lemonade stand coffee or Kurt Oppens' program notes, intermission gossip, crowds hoisting their programs as umbrellas, even parking lot dust, until one would have to agree with John Cage that music is everything that happens while the music lasts, or with John Muir that everything in the universe is hitched to everything else.

Behind the Tent's dismantling, incorporating half of the Paepcke parking lot, benches and other excreta were waiting to be hauled to unknown fates. A chainlink fence, installed overnight, guided the snoop to Harris Hall, whose lobby was open. There, rising from stacks of sealed cartons, stood the scale model of the Tent's Teflon replacement. Filled with matchstick benches and landscaped with wire trees, it was resting after a summer of soliciting donations. Canted, quadrangular, it resembled the apex of a Mayan pyramid. Beneath that fragile membrane, marooned among boxes waiting to be hauled away, lay the future of the Aspen Music Festival.

Afterword

IN THE SUMMER OF 1988 the editor of the program book asked me to write a history of the Aspen Music Festival for publication in the following year's program, part of the Festival's celebration of its upcoming fortieth anniversary. Having first attended the Festival as an awed kid in the mid-fifties, become an addicted adult who never missed a summer in over two decades, written magazine essays on the Festival that were included in my 1987 collection *Notes of A Half-Aspenite*, and chronically assaulted piano repertoire beyond my ability, I felt that I was the right choice for the task—yet the prospect daunted me. "That's a very long story," I replied. "What are the length limits?"

"There are none."

I wondered how much pulp Festival-goers were willing to support in their laps, but that was the Festival's call, not mine. I plunged in, interviewing dozens of musicians, patrons and Festival officials, many of whom I had never before had the chance to meet. Most were exceedingly gracious: one perennial star apologized that the Festival had cleared most of the amenities from her Red Mountain housing but she could offer me a choice of a Campari or a martini; another was so entranced by my own book-lined cabin, which transported her to the Aspen of her childhood, that conversation spiraled through excited reminiscence until she snapped, "Turn off that damned tape recorder so we can *really* talk."

During that period I spent winters at my mother's house outside Phoenix and there I retreated with tape transcripts, hoping to find their hidden design. The Festival's beginnings could be told year by year, but once the long trajectories of programming, the school, housing, concert facilities and the changing context of Aspen collided with the horizontal slices that were nine-week seasons, the narrative line wasn't so obvious. As I wrestled with this writerly dilemma my mother, who had reached the age of eighty in seemingly perfect health, suffered a heart attack and, ten days later, was gone. In the aftershock, facing the disposition of the house, the disposal of her possessions, my real wish was to study the cache of letters she had left: to review her life. But I had made a commitment to the Festival, felt I should act professionally even though I was a volunteer without a contract, and fought off the merely personal. At times grudgingly, I saw the material to its conclusion and got it in on time. Replied the editor who had requested it, "But this is much too long to fit in the program."

The editor did use the opening about the Goethe Bicentennial and ran the early year-by-year accounts as a forty-years-ago serialization. Then the story reached the blow-up between the musicians and Walter Paepcke. The event might be forty years old, with Paepcke himself more than two decades deceased, and every detail vouched for by sources on tape, but suggestions of Paepcke's authoritarian side were deemed too sensitive for public consumption. I continued writing for the program, that having become my way of participating in the music, but the history had become an envelope in a drawer.

I realized, however, that the fiftieth anniversary was approaching *accelerando*, that one more decade might chill old passions and that there still might be a use for the manuscript.

When Rudolph Firkušný passed through Aspen on what looked like a farewell tour, I snagged an interview. Asked to provide a capsule history of the Festival for the opening of Harris Hall, I condensed and updated the material. Finding myself in Paris in 1996 I called Madeleine Milhaud, then in her mid-nineties. I gave my name and explained my mission. "Come right over!" she gushed. "Every thought I have of Aspen is of you." While we had met once socially twenty years back, I couldn't imagine she recalled it and rode the *Métro* toward her apartment off Place Pigalle in considerable mystification. She buzzed me into the building, I knocked on her door and she gaped at me before asking me in. A brief exchange revealed that instead of Berger she had heard Berko, the Festival's first official photographer, a close friend she hadn't seen in twenty years and who was due to visit in two weeks.

"What did you think when you saw me?" I asked.

"My first thought was, my how Franz has changed!"

As the fiftieth anniversary approached, others were editing the program, running the Festival, and I let it be known that I had a history that they could publish to celebrate the half-century. I could interview further, update, fill in blanks: all I needed was assurance of publication and sufficient lead time. As years dwindled to months, the response was a cool perhaps and at one point it was reported back to me that "the Festival wants to look forward, not backward." So much, I thought, for the thousands of musicians and supporters who have gotten them to the present. Meanwhile I was gestating what loomed as a difficult book, a stew that made the horizontals and verticals of the Festival look like tic-tac-toe. I was chafing to begin and didn't want its composition interrupted. When publication of the Festival history finally seemed impossible, I started into the new project and worked murkily through the first passages until it started burning into the clear. Then came word that the Festival, with eight months until publication and less than that for a completed text, wanted the account of its past after all.

It was too late to involve an established publisher, too late to finance the book other than with advertisements. Because the project was approved after the 1998 season, it was also too late to interview more musicians, but Festival staff was still on hand and Lynn Harrell, whom I had not yet interviewed, remained in town, receiving therapy after his operation for carpal tunnel syndrome, and appeared at my house bearing a bottle of wine and a headful of stories.

Ernestine Ashley, publisher of *Sojourner,* a semi-annual hardback magazine distributed to Aspen hotel rooms, was summoned to pull the publication off. Ernie had been the founder of *Aspen Magazine,* had published my essays over the years, then collected them in *Half-Aspenite,* the magazine's only book, just before selling her publishing enterprise. It must be said that Ernie does her best work under pressure and that she and her staff—given the limitations of a hotel book format with encompassing ads—pulled off a coup in producing the book, called *A Tent in the Meadow,* on short notice. By the time editing was underway I was in La Paz, Baja California Sur, where I overwintered yearly after the death of my mother. Deadline fell before the last version was complete and I had to let Ernie's staff add data I was unable to blend into the narrative, let alone proofread. Ernie referred to the book as her "last miracle," and while I believe she has further miracles in reserve, miracle it was.

But certain miracles have their blemishes. Some readers were offended by the presence of advertising, the picky author wasn't thrilled with the wording of passages he didn't write and, most crucially, the account of the first fifty years didn't include the fiftieth summer itself, the summer the book was written for. When Johnson Books agreed to republish the history, less visually lavish, more textually complete, I sent a letter to three newspapers soliciting comments, emendations and complaints from those who had read the Festival version, and conducted yet more interviews. One musician found the account "too contentious, insufficiently celebratory." Another who had been brusquely dismissed from the Festival after a distinguished career said, "I'll correct the mistakes in what you've written, but you haven't told the real story."

"Is the real story political, not musical?" I asked.

"You bet."

Still another Festival associate faulted the text for showing the dark side of the Festival's past and not its present. I have written various books greater in length and scope, but no subject has been so determined to subvert its own portrait.

It has been my experience that arts organizations in Aspen—and, by report, in the rest of the world—are obsessively at each other's throats and devour their own. While jockeying for power that is mostly symbolic may be characteristic of the human race at large, it seems disproportionately vicious among the subset that gravitates to the arts. An account that ignores the scheming shortchanges reality, but there would be nothing to scheme over if it were not for the art in question.

Writing about a pioneering institution that has involved thousands of musicians over a half-century is like shining a flashlight in the British Museum. A more complete account of the Aspen Music Festival remains to be written and I will be its eager reader, not its writer. I have kept myself out of the account until this indulgent afterword, but as a compulsive observer for more than half of the Festival's life I have imbued it, for better or worse, with my fixations and sensibility. In a nonverbal core beyond politics lies the music itself which, even at its most tragic, expresses imagination, craft, and a sheer determination to be heard that overcomes all passing pettiness to generate joy.

Aspen
October 2000

Executives and Trustees

1954–1999

Note: December 17, 1954 was the first official meeting of the Board of Trustees.

Executive Directors and Presidents

Richard P. Leach, 1953
Norman Singer, 1954–62
James Cain, 1963–67
Gordon Hardy, 1968–89
Robert Harth, 1990 to present

Board of Trustees

Adele Addison, 1986–88
Thea Adelson, 1996 to present
Nancy Allen, 1996 to present
George Anderman, 1988–93
Diane Anderson, 1998 to present
Lester Anderson, 1986–94, Life Trustee
   1995 to present
Thomas Anderson, 1992–96
Sue Anschutz-Rodgers, 1998 to present
Dr. Karl Arndt, 1964–72
Nadine Asin, 1989–96
Mrs. Marshall Barnard, 1963–68
Courtlandt D. Barnes, 1954–81,
   Life Trustee 1990–97
Peter Bay, 1987–88
Joella Bayer, 1956–63
Frederic A. Benedict, 1962–93,
   Life Trustee 1994–95
Edward Berkeley, 1994 to present
Dr. Paula Bernstein, 1992–98
Dr. William Bernstein, 1974–91
Carl Bickert, 1992 to present
Kate Blakely, 1959–68
Per Brevig, 1989–90
William Broeder, 1998 to present
Katherine Buchanan, 1989–90
Matthew Bucksbaum, 1985 to present
James Bulkley, 1986
William E. Burwell, 1993 to present
Connie Calaway, 1996 to present
Harry Campbell, 1987–91
Heidi Castleman, 1996 to present
Jessica Catto, 1973–80

John Cerminaro, 1987–90
James J. Chaffin, 1981–85
Merle C. Chambers, 1994 to present
Franklin A. Chanen, 1994 to present
Tina Chen-Josephson, 1986–92
Stephen Clapp, 1979–90
Louise N. Clow, 1969–71
Nick Coates, 1997 to present
Mrs. Charles Collier, 1960–61
Randolph Colman, 1984–85
Noël R. Congdon, 1988 to present
Barbara K. Conviser, 1980–85
Mrs. George Cranmer, 1956–63
Paula H. Crown, 1989–95,
   1996 to present
Michael Czajkowski, 1989–90, 1991–95
Marian Lyeth Davis, 1967–68,
   Life Trustee 1990 to present
Dorothy DeLay, 1981–84, 1986–93,
   Honorary Trustee 1990 to present
Edward H. Deming, 1974–82
John Denver, 1975–80
Alfred J. Dietsch, 1992–97,
   1998 to present
John F. Doremus, Jr., 1959–83,
   Life Trustee 1996 to present
Sutherland Dows, Jr., 1974–82
Caroline W. Duell, 1986–1991
Bil Dunaway, 1996 to present
Harold Feder, 1986–91
Nathan P. Feinsinger, 1954–75,
   Life Trustee 1976–83
William Field, 1956–67
James Fifield, 1995 to present
Dr. Giles F. Filley, 1986–88
David M. Fleisher, 1989–93
Martin Flug, 1983–85, 1992–95,
   1997 to present
Revill J. Fox, 1971–76
Opal Fultz, 1960–79, Life Trustee 1980–86
Rosemary Furman, 1992–98
Leonard Gertler, 1993 to present
John C. Ginn, 1981
David Gitlitz, 1998 to present
Michael A. Goldberg, 1993 to present
Szymon Goldberg, Life Trustee 1980
Esther Goodrich, 1955–62

143

Aspen Music Festival and School

Artist-Faculty, Composers-in-Residence, Visiting Composers, and Guest Artists
1949–1999

* = Alumnae
† = Music Director

Martha Aarons
Geulah Abrahams
Charles Abramovic
Claus Adam
David Adams
John Adams
Adele Addison
Bernard Adelstein
Thomas Adès
Samuel Adler
Bruce Adolphe*
Angella Ahn*
Lucia Ahn*
Maria Ahn*
Ahn Trio*
Anthony Aibel*
Hugh Aitken
Nami Akimatsu
Toshiko Akiyoshi
Albeneri Trio
Eunice Alberts
Theo Alcantara
John Aler*
John Aley
Nancy Allen*
Frank Almond*
Harry Alshin
Marin Alsop
Christian Altenburger*
Amadeus Quartet
Carol Stein Amado
Amati Trio
Elly Ameling
American Brass Quintet
American String Quartet*
Alison Ames

Gilbert Amy
Einar Anderson*
Elizabeth Anderson*
Carol Anderson
Leif Ove Andsnes
Alexander Anisimov
Adele Anthony*
Apple Hill Chamber
  Players*
Atar Arad
Renata Arado
Charlene Archibèque
Stewart Arfman*
Dominick Argento
Arista Trio
Karan Armstrong
Leonard Arner
Claudio Arrau
Lydia Artymiw
Jerome Ashby*
Daniel Asia
Nadine Asin*
Aspen Woodwind
  Quintet*
Odair Assad
Sergio Assad
Lynne Aspnes
David Atherton
Edward Auer*
Arleen Auger
Larry Austin
Norma Auzin
Daniel Avshalomov*
Jacob Avshalomov
Emanuel Ax
Yoko Ax
Kees van Baaren
Victor Babin
Andreas Bach

Richard Bado
Grace Mihi Bahng*
Simon Bainbridge
James Baker
Leonardo Balada
Dalton Baldwin
Wesley Balk
Joan Balter
Carmen Balthrop
Julian Barber
Randall Bare
Raymond Barker
Edward Barnes
Richard Barrett*
Leon Barzin
Robert Bass
Stephen Basson*
Earle Bates
Jeanne Baxtresser*
Peter Bay*
J.R. Beardsley
Robert Beaser
Ray Bechenstein
Robert Becker*
Fred Begun
Jan Behr
Joshua Bell*
William Bell
Louie Bellson
David Bender
Jeffrey Benedict*
Jack Benny
Daniel Benyamini
Ara Berberian
Erich Bergel
Theodor Berger
Scott Bergeson
Luciano Berio
Edward Berkeley

147

Paul Berl
Mario Bernardi
Barbara Bernhard
Greg Berton
Robert Biddlecome
Jeffrey Biegel
Carolyn Bilderback
Edward Birdwell
Jeanette Bittar
Dierdre Black
Robert Black
Helen Blackburn
Joy Blackett*
Justice Harry A.
  Blackmun
Virgil Blackwell*
Florence Blager
Blair String Quartet
Stephen Blier
Michel Block
Herbert Blomstedt
Myron Bloom
Robert Bloom
Hamiet Bluett
Aaron Bodenhorn
Florent Boffard
John Paul Bogart
Thomas Bogdan*
William Bolcom*
Ann Bollinger
Maurice Bonney
Michael Bookspan
Carel Boomkamp
Victor Borge
Ronard Borror
Leon Botstein
Richard Bower
Harold Boxer
Bonita Boyd
Boys of the Colorado
  Children's Chorus
Edward Bradley
Gwendolyn Bradley
Alexander Braginsky
Norbert Brainin
Evelyne Brancart
Alice Brandfonbrener
Bruce Bransby*
Henry Brant
Julie Braun
Karen Branzell
Sonny Bravo
Per Brevig
Carter Brey
Nick Brignola
Benjamin Britten

Yefim Bronfman
Barry Brook
Patricia Brooks
Tamara Brooks*
Zelman Brounoff
Earle Brown
Helen Brown
Keith Brown
Ray Brown
Katherine Brubaker
Garnett Bruce
Philip Brunelle
Karen Brunssen
Anshel Brusilow
Jane Brydon*
Richard Buckley
David Burge
Mary Burgess
Sam Burtis
Gary Burton
Jon Busch*
Sam Bush
Barry Busse
James Busterud*
Don Butterfield
Leone Buyse
Charlie Byrd
John Cahill
James Caldwell
Paul Callaway
Stuart Canin
Jody Cardamone
Tom Cardamone
Claudine Carlson
Earl Carlyss*
Laurie Carney*
Norman Carol
Bob Carpenter
Catherine Carroll*
Elliott Carter
Carol Castel
Nico Castel
Heidi Castleman
Saul Caston†
Ronald Catalbiano
Javier Cendejas*
Charlotte Cerminaro*
John Cerminaro*
Leslie Chabay
James Chambers
David Chan*
Sonia Chan*
Dorothy Chang
Min Soo Chang
Sarah Chang*
Peiwen Chao

Yves Chardon
Michael Charry
Carlos Chávez
John Cheek
Edith Chen*
Robert Chen*
Chen Yi
Marietta Cheng*
Gloria Cheng-Cochran*
Victoria Chiang
Catherine Cho*
Gabriel Chodos
Colorado Children's
  Chorale
Sang-Mi Chung
Julie Churchill*
Kristine Ciesinski
Giorgio Ciompi
Stephen Clapp
Classic Chorale of
  Denver
Fred Clem
Cleveland Quartet
Daryl Coad*
Kevin Cobb
Pamela Coburn*
Jean-David Coen*
Jeff Coffin
Chad Cognata*
Franklin Cohen*
Isidore Cohen
Paul Cohen
Robert Cohen
Roger Cole
Peter Coleman-Wright
Judy Collins
Colorado Symphony
  Chorus
Evelina Colorni
Katherine Collier
Catherine Comet*
Sergiu Comissiona
Ruth Condon*
James Conlon*
Carol Conrad
Fiora Contino
Deborah Cook
Joseph Cook
Claudia Coonce*
Paul Cooper
Roberta Cooper
Julia Copeland
Aaron Copland
Rebecca Copley*
John Corigliano
Eugene Corporon

Larry Coryell
Marcel Couraud
Carole Cowan*
Daniel Craik*
Margaret Cramer
Trudy Ellen Craney
Donald Crockett
George Crumb
Gilda Cruz-Romo
Phyllis Curtin
Michael Czajkowski*
Luigi Dallapiccola
Paul Daniel
Richard Danielpour
Eddie Daniels
Stephen Dankner
Blythe Danner
Michael Dash*
Michael Daugherty
Mario Davidovsky
Randall Davidson
Dennis Russell Davies*
Sir Peter Maxwell Davies
Robert Davine
Douglas Davis
Jon Deak*
Warren Deck
Marcella DeCray
Doreen DeFeis*
Jan DeGaetani
Wilfredo Deglans*
Steven De Groote
Nap De Klijn
Louis Herrera
de la Fuente
John De Lancie, Sr.
John De Lancie, Jr.
Alicia de Larrocha
Dorothy DeLay
Joseph DeLeon
Andreas Delfs*
Alfred Deller
Norman Dello Joio
Arthur Delmoni*
Gaetano Delogu
Sergio de los Cobos
David Del Tredici*
Marjorie DeLuca
John DeMain
Frederic de Marseille
Brian Dembow*
Deng
Patrick Denniston
John Denver*
Denver Symphony

Orchestra
James DePreist
Vincent de Rosa
William DeRosa*
Rohan De Silva*
Nicholas Deutch
William DeVan*
Edo de Waart
Michelle DeYoung
David Diamond
Andrés Diaz
Antonio Diaz
Justino Diaz
Steven Dibner*
Cipa Dichter
Misha Dichter
Dichter-McDuffie-
Kirshbaum Trio
James Dickson
Glen Dicterow*
Vincent DiMartino
Tonio Di Paolo*
Eileen Dishinger*
Ronald Dishinger*
Michele Djokic*
Daniel Domb
Felix Donaldson
William Dooley
Dorothy Dorow
Elaine Douvas
Jeaneane Dowis*
Everett Drake
Eugene Drucker*
Jacob Druckman
Rafael Druian
Gail Dubinbaum*
Marilyn Dubow*
George Dudea
Chris Dudley
Richard Dufallo
Cloyd Duff
Erika Duke
Stephen Dumaine
Mary Duncan
James Dunham*
Paul Dunkel*
Louis Dunoyer
de Segonzac
Hank Dutt
Lawrence Dutton*
John Duykers
Richard Dyer-Bennet
David Dzubay
Charles Eakin
John Eargle
Julius Eastman

John Eaton
Douglas Edelman
William Eddins
Timothy Eddy
Sian Edwards
David Effron
Joseph Eger
Akira Eguchi*
Sixten Ehrling
Bruno Eicher
Saul Eichner
Thomas F. Eirman
Michelle Ekizian
Mark Elder
Bobby Eledredge
Karen Eley*
Jens Ellerman
Duke Ellington
Anthony Elliott*
Brent Ellis*
Paul Ellison
Emerson String Quartet
Mary Endress
Elizabeth Enkells*
Pamela Epple*
Alvin Epstein
Paul Epstein
Donald Erb
Stephen Erdody*
Kaaren Erickson
Broadus Erle
Eroica Trio
Jocelyn Estep*
Cynthia Estill*
Toshiya Eto
August Everding
Eric Ewazen
Jimmy Fadden
JoAnn Falletta*
Philip Farkas
Carole Farley
Ellen Faull
José Feghali
Ilona Feher
Yosif Feigelson
Michael Feinstein
David Felder
Vladimir Feltsman
Janice Felty
Bruce Ferden
John Ferillo
Bruno Ferrandis*
Daniel Ferro
Festival Quartet
Julie Feves*
Sally Field
Rafael Figueroa

Steven Finch
David Finckel
Fine Arts Quartet
Ian Finkel
Rudolph Firkušný
Ivan Fischer
Eliot Fisk*
William Fitzpatrick*
Béla Fleck
Béla Fleck and the
  Flecktones
Elizabeth Fleischer*
Leon Fleisher
Renée Fleming*
Samuel Flor
Carlisle Floyd*
Dan Fogelberg
Charles Foidart
Helen Foli
Lea Foli
Carl Fontana
Andrew Ford
Maureen Forrester
Lukas Foss
Herbert Foster
Lawrence Foster*†
Martin Foster*
Robert Fountain
Malcom Frager
Hal France
Mikko Franck
Claude Frank
Peter Frankl
Free Flight
Robert Freeman
Adolphe Frezin
Glen Frey
Paul Fried
David Friedman*
Götz Friedrich
Jerrold Frohmader
Ellen Frohnmayer
Philip Frohnmayer
Paul Fromm
Arnold Fromme
Daniel Froschauer*
Thomas Frost
Lillian Fuchs
Curtis Fuller
Mimmi Fulmer
Marjorie Fulton
Future Man
George Gaber
James Galway
Isabel Ganz*
Raya Garbousova

Robert Gardner
Bernard Garfield
David Garvey
John Garvey
David Geber*
Chris Gekker
Saida Gerrard
Grant Gershon*
Gordon Getty
Oscar Ghiglia
Marion Gibson*
Alan Gilbert
Daniel Gilbert
Pia Gilbert
James Gilmer
Shirley Givens
Detlev Glanert
Philip Glass*
Herta Glaz
Rosemary Glyde*
Ken Godel
Paul Godwin
Alexander Goehr
Nancy Goeres
Szymon Goldberg†
Lauren Goldstein*
Albert Goltzer
Harold Goltzer
Eddie Gomez
Rubén González
Karen Gomyo*
Bradley Goode*
Benny Goodman
Barnard Goodman
Saul Goodman
George Goslee
Stephen Gosling
Howard Gottlieb
Victor Gottlieb
Phillip Gottling*
Mark Gould
Hans Graf
Uta Graf
Gary Graffman
John Graham
Robin Graham*
Donald Gramm
Riley Grannen
Johanna Graudan
Nicholai Graudan
Gary Gray*
George Gray
Kathryn Greenbank*
Herbert Greenberg
Noah Greenberg
Willie Greene

Jodi Greitzer*
Judson Griffin*
Walter Griffith
Hélène Grimaud
Neal Gripp
Murray Grodner
Michael Groniger
Robert Gross
Thomas Grossenbacher
Jerry Grossman*
Larry Grossman
Thomas Grubb
William Grubb*
Eugenie Grunewald
David Grusin
Irene Gubrud*
Marion Guest
Leslie Guinn
Robert Guthrie
Ara Guzelimian
Armen Guzelimian
Seung-Un Ha*
Jonathan Haas
Pia Haas
John Hagen
Matt Haimovitz*
Thomas Haines
Richard Halajian
Victor von Halem
Laurel Hall
William Hall
Carl Halvorson*
David Hamilton
David Hammond
Vinson Hammond*
"Slide" Hampton
Yehuda Hanani
Jeff Hanna
Per Hannevold
Koichiro Harada*
John Harbison
Rose Mary Harbison
Gordon Hardy
Alan Harler
Lynn Harrell*
Mack Harrell
David Harrington
Jan Harrington
Alan Harris
Eddie Harris
Emmylou Harris
Matthew Harris
Lou Harrison
Don Harry
William Harry
Margaret Harshaw

Sidney Harth
Teresa Harth
Richard Hartshorne*
Ellen Hassman*
Inez Hassman*
Lenore Hatfield*
Michael Hatfield*
Betty Hauk
Stephen Hawking
Margaret Hawkins
William Hawley
Hawthorne String Quartet
Lorna Haywood*
Scott Healy
Constance Heard*
Jimmy Heath
Daniel Hege
Benar Heifetz
Hans Heinz
Alan Held
Claude Helffer
Jaquiline Helin
Andrew Heller*
William Hellerman
Eddie Henderson
Joe Henry
Jane Henschel*
Bev R. Hensen
Hans Werner Henze
Phyllis Herdliska
Julius Herford
Benjamin Herman*
Alice Hermes
Paul Hersh
Ralph Hersh
Norman Herzberg
John Hicks
Douglas Hill
John Hill
Nancy Hill*
Margaret Hillis
Raphael Hillyer
Jerome Hines
Fred Hinger
Jun'ichi Hirokami
Grayson Hirst*
Cecilia Hobbs*
William Hobbs
Jim Hodgkinson*
Sydney Hodkinson
Debbie Hoffman
Gary Hoffman
Linda Hohenfeld
Richard Holmes*
Karen Holvik*
Bridgett Hooks

Hans Hotter
Stephen Hough
Douglas Howard
Inda Howland
Milton Howorth
Si-Jing Huang
Judith Hubbell*
Harry Huff
Robert Hufstader
Alexandra Hughes
Katherine Hughes
Duane Hulbert*
Kees Hulsmann
John Humphrey
Hungarian String Quartet
John Hunt
Karel Husa
Brian Hymel
Jimmy Ibbotson
Michael Iceberg
Alan Iglitzin
Irving Ilmer
Nobuko Imai*
Craig Impink
International Sejong
    Soloists
Jeffrey Irvine*
Johnathan Irving*
Robert Irving
Sharon Isbin*
Eugene Istomin
Ko Iwasaki
Paavo Järvi
Bil Jackson*
Tiffany Jackson*
Paul Jacoby
Jane Vial Jaffe
Peter Jaffe*
Dennis James*
Byron Janis
David Janower*
Georges Janzer
John Jarvis
Peter Jarvis
Kenneth Jean*
Joan Jeanrenaud
Paul Jeffrey
Barry Jekowsky*
Daven Jenkins*
Grant Johannesen
Jennifer John*
Beverly Peck Johnson
Michael Chase Johnson
Ben Johnston
Elissa Johnston*
David Jolley*

Bronwen Jones
Charles Jones
Sheila Jordan
James Judd
Vasile Jucan
Juilliard String Quartet
Doris Jung
Vic Juris
Donald Kaasch
Erich Itor Kahn
Irene Kahn
Morris Kainuma*
Joseph Kalichstein
Kalichstein-Laredo-
    Robinson Trio
Gilbert Kalish
Lilian Kallir
Michael Kamen*
Wally Kane
Hyo Kang*
Paul Kantor*
Mark Kaplan*
Nicholas Kapros
Isaac Karabtchevsky
Gary Karr*
Kim Kashkashian
George Kast*
Stephen Kates*
Albert Katz
Helen Katz*
Martha Strongin Katz
Paul Katz
Leonidas Kavakos
Fumiko Kawasaki*
Masao Kawasaki*
Danny Kaye
Donald Keats
Robert Keefe
Christopher Keene
Alan Kefauver
Garrison Keillor
Reginald Kell
Judith Kellock
Roger Kelloway
Gary Kendall
Joe Kennedy, Jr.
Nigel Kennedy*
Aaron Jay Kernis
Alexander Kerr
Myra Kestenbaum*
Julia Kierstine
Kenneth Kiesler
Carson Kievman
Richard Killmer
Benny Kim*
Earl Kim

Eric Kim*
Min Sun Kim
Young Uk Kim
Yuri Kim
John King
Freya Kirby*
Leon Kirchner
Ralph Kirshbaum
Paul Klemme*
Werner Klemperer
Joe Kloess
Thomas Knab
Ernest Knell*
Jack Knitzer
Amy Knoles
Sato Knudsen
Oliver Knussen
Daniel Kobialka
Mari Kodama
Robert Koenig
Robert Koff*
Judith Kogan
Roland Kohloff
Toshiko Kohno*
Terri Koide
Varujan Kojian
Barbara Kolb
Lee Konitz
Patricia Kopec*
Florence Kopleff
Dénes Koromzay
Karl Korte
Mark Kosower*
Stephen Kovacevich
William Kraft
David Krakauer*
Jonathan D. Kramer
Lili Kraus
Tom Krause
Jacalyn Bower Kreitzer
Yakov Kreizberg
Elena Kremer
Gidon Kremer
KREMERata BALTICA
Ernst Krenek
Matthias Kriesberg
Kronos Quartet
Joel Krosnick
Paul Krzywicki*
Adam Kuenzel
Anton Keurti
Meyer Kupferman
Michael Kuttner
Yoon Kyung Kwon*
Kathryn LaBouff
Fredell Lack

Leopold Lafosse
Gary Lakes
Sara Lambert*
Maria Lambros*
Julie Landsman*
Burl Lane*
David Lang
David Langlitz
Jack Lanning*
Paul Lansky
Jaime Laredo
Ruth Laredo
Libby Larson
Albert Laszlo
Jacob Lateiner
Laurien Laufman
Herbert Laws
Joel Lazar*
Roy Lazarus
Richard Leacock
Evelyn Lear
Ann LeBaron
Sung-Ju Lee*
Yura Lee*
Benjamin Lees
Ronan Lefkowitz
Erich Leinsdorf*
Paula Lenchner
John A. Lennon
Lenox Quartet
Kathleen Lenski*
Ronald Leonard
Jerald Lepinski
Edmond LeRoy*
Christopher Leuba
Joel Levi
Ida Levin
Robert Levin
James Levine*
Bruce Levington*
Eugene Levinson
Gerald Levinson
Gina Levinson
Nanette Levy
Philip Levy
Arthur Lewis*
Daniel Lewis
Harmon Lewis
J. Reilly Lewis
Rosina Lhévinne
Cecile Licad
Mats Lidstrom
Samuel Lifschey
Peter Lightfoot
Espen Lillislatten
Elizabeth Lim*

Cho-Liang Lin*
Wesley Lindskoog
Jahja Ling
Michael Lipman
Samuel Lipman
John Lithgow
Andrew Litton
Arthur Loesser
Abraham Loft
Timothy Long*
Daniel Lordon*
Robin Lorenz
Yvonne Loriod
Lyle Lovett
Martin Lovett
Sergiu Luca
Humbert Lucarelli
Alvin Lucier
Alice Ludine
Mark Ludwig
Witold Lutoslawski
Lee Luvisi
Yo-Yo Ma
Salvatore Macchia
Robert MacDonald
Tod Machover
Sir Charles Mackerras
Stephen Mackey
José Madera
James Maddalena
Teiko Maehashi
Samuel Magad
Vince Lawrence Maggio
Gabriel Magyar
Kaitlin Mahoney*
Maia Quartet*
Spiro Malas
Barbara Mallow
Russell Malone
Nicholas Mann*
Robert Mann
Elizabeth Mannion
Theodora Mantz
Adele Marcus
John Marcus
Nadine Markanian
Wynton Marsalis
Peter Marsh
Steve Marsh
Cheryl Marshall
Ingram Marshall
Mike Marshall
Barbara Ann Martin*
Philip Martin
Vincent Martino
Raymond Mase

William Masselos
Kathleen Mattis
Nancy Maultsby
Dorothy Maynor
Priscilla McAfee*
Donald McCall
Patricia McCarty
Bruce McClellen*
John McCollum
Seth McCoy
Ron McCroby
Robert McDuffie*
Bobby McFerrin
Nicholas McGegan
Paul McKee
Matt McKenzie
Sylvia McNair*
Brent McNunn*
Myron McPherson
Marilyn Mead*
Barbara Ann Meek*
Kurt Meisenbach*
Lauritz Melchior
Meliora String Quartet*
Jackie Melnick
Men of the Colorado
    Symphony Chorus
Pierre Menard
Mendelssohn Quartet
Antonio Meneses
Peter Mennin
Susanne Mentzer
Robert Merfeld*
Michael Mermagen*
Kenneth Merrill
Olivier Messiaen
Jorge Mester*†
Edgar Meyer*
Anne Akiko Meyers*
Janice Meyerson
Edna Michelle
Midori*
Butch Miles
Piotr Milewski*
Darius Milhaud
Madeleine Milhaud
Mladen Milicevic*
David Allen Miller
Forrestt Miller*
Robert Miller
Aprille Millo
Nathan Milstein
Minneapolis Symphony
    Orchestra
Minnesota Chorale
Shlomo Mintz*

Bobby Mintzer
Mischa Mischakoff
Abraham Mishkind
Irina Mishure
Danlee Mitchell
Dimitri Mitropoulos†
James Mobberly
James Moffitt*
Gaetano Molieri
Thelonious Monk, Jr.
Carlos Montoya
Dudley Moore
James Moore
Lisa Moore
Oskar Morawetz
Jean Morel
David Morelock
Daniel Morganstern
Erica Morini
Gareth Morrell
Joan Morris
Theodore Morrison
Steven Morscheck*
John Moses
Karen Moses*
Stephen Mosko
William Moylan
Donald Muggeridge
Hanna-Lora Muller
Simon Mulligan
Jeffrey Mumford*
Thomas Muraco*
Katherine Murdock
Shawn Murphy
Wayne Murry
Walt Myers
Fredric Myrow
Nicholas Nabokov
Kent Nagano
Robert Nagel
Elemer Nagy
Ryohei Nakagawa
Susan Narucki
Makiko Narumi
John Nauman
Craig Naylor*
Martin Neary
Buell Neidlinger*
Marc Neikrug
Anton Nel
John Nelson*
Ron Nelson
Zara Nelsova
Netherlands String
    Quartet
New Music String

Quartet
New York Pro Musica
New York Saxophone
    Quartet
New York String Quartet
Beth Newdome
Hans Newfield
John Newfield
Anthony Newman
Susan Nicholson
Kurt Nikkanen*
Joaquin Nin-Culmel
Siegmund Nissel
Barbara Nissman
Nitty Gritty Dirt Band
Judith Norell*
Arne Nordheim
Jerold Norman
Bruce Norris*
Mary Norris
Bärli Nugent*
John Obetz
Eugene O'Brien
Mark O'Connor
Tara Helen O'Connor
David Oei*
Garrick Ohlsson
Junko Ohtsu*
Theodore Oien*
Elmar Oliveira
Jan Opalach*
Opera Colorado Chorus
Edith Oppens
Kurt Oppens
Ursula Oppens*
Christopher O'Riley*
Richard Ormrod*
Doris Ornstein
Orion String Quartet
Peter Orth
Robert Orth*
Paul Ostrovsky*
David Ostwald
Deborah Overton
Charles Owen
Paganini String Quartet
Robert Page
Emmanuel Pahud
Alexander Paley
Ray Pankratz*
Cecilia Papendick
Alyssa Park*
Julia Park*
Laura Park*
Tricia Park*
Alice Parker

William Parker
Zaidee Parkinson
Leslie Parnas
Harry Partch Ensemble
Thomas Pasatieri*
Larry Passin
Joseph Passaro
György Pauk
Pamela Paul*
Thomas Paul
Stephen Paulson
Anders Paulsson*
Stephen Paulus
Richard Pearlman
Thomas Peck
John Pedroja*
Carmen Pelton*
Krzysztof Penderecki
Pendulum
Guilliermo Perich
Itzhak Perlman
Navah Perlman*
Alcestis Perry*
Antoinette Perry*
David Perry*
Herbert Perry
John Perry
Julia Perry
Robert Perry*
Vincent Persichetti
Rolf Persinger
Alexander Peskanov*
Mark Peskanov*
John E. Pfeiffer
Daniel Phillips
Harvey Phillips
Todd Phillips
Uri Pianka
Gregor Piatigorsky
Tobiaz Picker
Evelino Pido
Ted Piltzecker*
Howard Pink*
Walter Piston
Harvey Pittel
Bucky Pizzarelli
Carol Plantamura
Russell Platt
Mikhail Pletnyov
Anthony Plog
Kathryn Plummer*
Vincent Plush
Sylvia Plyler
Joseph Polisi
Paul Polivnick*
Claudia Polley

Leon Pommers
Bernard Pommier
Walter Ponce
Felix Popper
Bob Porcelli
Leonard Posner
Michael Powell
Awadagin Pratt
Michael Pratt*
William Preucil
Paul Price
Penelope Price-Jones
Brian Priestman
William Primrose
Pro Arte Consort
James Progris
Tito Puente
Jimmy Pugh
Pamela Pyle*
Thomas Pyle
Florence Quivar
Milenko Rado
Larry Rachleff
Matthew Raimondi
Ron Raines
David Ramadanoff*
Lynn Ramsey-Irvine*
Shulamit Ran
Bernard Rands
Thomas Raney
Louis Ranger
Behzad Ranjbaran
Herbert Rankin
Kenny Rankin
Jim Ratts
Leonard Raver
Tim Ray
Curtis Rayam*
Francine Reed
Gustave Reese
Al Regni
Bill Reichenbach
Buck Reid
Aribert Reimann
Alice Rejto
Gabor Rejto
Peter Rejto*
John Relyea
Tanya Remenikova
Joel Revzen*
Samuel Rhodes*
William Rhodes
Ruggiero Ricci
Thomas Riebl
Kenneth Riegel
Vittorio Rieti

Fritz Rikko
Helmuth Rilling
Jennifer Ringo*
William Ritchen
Karen Ritscher
Mario Rivera
Sandra Rivers*
Marcus Roberts
Christopher Robertson
David Robertson
Sandra Robbins*
Faye Robinson
Sharon Robinson
George Rochberg
Claudio Roditi
Bobby Rodriguez
John Rodriguez
Piro Rodriguez
Robert Xavier Rodriguez
Noël Rogers
Jim Rohrig
John Rojak
Jean-Marc Rollez
Neil Rolnick*
Gustavo Romero*
Rebecca Root*
Ned Rorem
Ellen Rose*
Leonard Rose
Ronald Roseman
Mary Rosen
Nathaniel Rosen
Michael Rosenberg
Sylvia Rosenberg*
Joseph Rosenstock†
Anthony Ross
Walter Ross
Gustave Rosseels
Sarah Rothenberg
Christopher Rouse
Lucy Rowan
Tracy Rowell
Royale Trio
Arthur Rubinstein
Julius Rudel
Phillip Ruder*
Robert Rudie
Paul Rudy
Franz Rupp
Rosemary Russell*
Leon Russianoff
James Ryan
Pamela Ryan*
Boris Rybka
Steven Rydberg
James Ryon

Olga Ryss
Joel Sachs
Michael Sachs
Carl Sakofsky
Peter Salaff
Nadja Salerno-
    Sonnenberg*
Jim Salestrom
Aulis Sallinen
David Sampson
Brent Samuel
Leonard Samuels
Howard Sandroff
Le Ting Sankey
Stuart Sankey*
Mischa Santora*
Richard Sarpola
Kurt Sassmannshaus*
Atsuko Sato*
Eriko Sato
Yuna Sato*
Angela Satris*
Henri Sauguet
Bryan Savage
Peter Schat
Ann Schein
Kenneth Schermerhorn
Peter Schickele*
Peter Schidlof
Askel Schiotz
Lauren Schiff
Martha Schlamme*
Sanford Schonbuch
Eva-Christina
    Schönweiss*
Robert Schoppert
Daniel Schorr
Yizhak Schotten
Jaap Schroeder
Mark Schroeder*
André-Michel Schub
Gunther Schuller
Elizabeth Schulze*
William Schuman
Gerard Schwarz*
Hans Schwieger†
James Schwisow
Claudio Scimone
Stephen Scott
Peter Sculthorpe
Sir Humphrey Searle
Denis Sedov
Gilbert Seeley
Uri Segal
Leif Segerstam*
Paula Seibel*

Peter Sellars
Jerzy Semkow
Keith Seppanen
John Serry
John Sessions
Roger Sessions
Philip Setzer
Doc Severinson
Lawrence Shader*
Gil Shaham*
Orli Shaham*
David Shallon
Stacy Shames*
Rita Shane*
Bud Shank
Ravi Shankar
Ralph Shapey
Eudice Shapiro
Maurice Sharp
William Sharp*
Leonard Sharrow
Marlena Shaw
Robert Shaw
George Shearing
Howard Shelley
Lucy Shelton*
Bright Sheng
Thomas Z. Shepard
John Sherba
Robert Sherman
Jonathan Sherwin
Bobby Shew
Lisa Shihoten
Ayako Shinozaki*
Ora Shiran*
George Shirley
Joseph Shore*
David Shostac
Maxim Shostakovich
Arlene Shrut
Matthew Shubin*
Lan Shui
Alan Shulman
Harry Shulman
Leonard Shure
Murry Sidlin*
Corky Siegel
Jeffrey Siegel
Joshua Siegel*
Nicusor Silaghi
Jasha Silberstein
Faye-Ellen Silverman
Joseph Silverstein
Leopold Simoneau
Martial Singhert
Kresimir Sipusch

Jerry Sirucek
Abraham Skernick
James Skoog
Stanislaw Skrowaczewski
Leonard Slatkin*
Rita Sloan*
Joel Smirnoff
Brooks Smith
Larry Alan Smith*
Lawrence Leyton Smith
Linda Smith
Martin Smith*
Martin Smith
Norman Smith*
Rohan Smith
Stephanie Smith
Wayne Foster Smith
W. Stephen Smith
Page Smith-Weaver
Dennis Smylie*
Peter Snell
Amy Snyder
Barry Snyder
Livia Sohn*
Lew Soloff
Izler Solomon†
Lee Soper*
Leonard Sorkin
Naomi Sorkin
David Soyer
Robert Spano
Mark Sparks
Marylou Speaker*
Paul Sperry*
Robert Spillman
Carlton Sprague-Smith
Dan Spurlock*
Gloria Spurlock*
Maria Stader
Marvin Stamm
Geoffrey Stanton
Sheryl Staples
Robert Starer
Paulina Stark
Starling Chamber
    Orchestra
David Starobin
Kathleen Starr
Eleanor Steber
Laurie Steele
Ainar Steen-Nöckleberg
Rand Steiger
Leonard Stein
William Steinberg†
Marjorie Steiner
Robert Stephenson

Isaac Stern
Michael Stern
Mitchell Stern*
Herbert Stessin
Nancy Stessin
John Stevens*
Susan Stevens
Alexander Stevenson
Mark Stewart
Thomas Stewart
David Ogden Stiers
Ray Still
Stephen Stills
William L. Stirling
James Stith
Dorothy Stone
William Stone
Ian Strasfogel
Igor Stravinsky
Lee Strawn*
Ron Streicher
Mark Stringer*
Rebecca Stout*
Susan Stubbs*
Thomas Stubbs*
Neal Stulberg*
Eric Stumacher*
Sally Stunkel
Marius Suarasan
Elier Suarez
Morton Subotnick*
Stephen Sulich
Cornelius Sullivan*
Conrad Susa
William Susman
Walter Susskind†
Kishiko Suzumi
Howard Swan
Fredrick Swann
Harvie Swartz
Ian Swenson*
Joseph Swenson*
Warren Swenson
Yi-Kwei Sze
Zoltán Székély
Lew Tabackin
Takács String Quartet
Kyoko Takezawa*
Yoav Talmi
Naoko Tanaka*
Buddy Tate
Grady Tate
Billy Taylor
Billy Taylor Trio
Rose Taylor
Ross Taylor

Steven Taylor*
Chris Teal
Henri Temianka
Yuri Temirkanov
Steven Tenenbom
James Tenney
Leopold Teraspulsky
Robert Termine*
Terra Australis Incognita
Clark Terry
Markand Thakar
Sabina Thatcher
Gaudencio Thiago
   de Mello
Andrew Thomas*
Augusta Read Thomas*
Elmer Thomas
Michael Tilson Thomas
Nancy Thomas*
Viviane Thomas*
David Thompson
Don Thompson
Harvey Thompson
Marcus Thompson*
Robert Thompson*
Virgil Thomson
Donald Thulean
Sir Michael Tippett
Albert Tipton
Richard Titelbaum
Dave Tofani
Dan Tomlinson
Alexander Toradze
Abe Torchinsky
Brian Torff*
Werner Torkanowsky
Michael Torke*
Mel Tormé
Mel Tormé Trio
Yan Pascal Tortelier
Roman Totenberg
Jennie Tourel
Joan Tower*
Walter Trampler
Transylvan Quartet
Yaron Traub
Helen Traubel
Michael Tree
Charles Treger
Stephanie Tretick
Michael Trimble*
George Tsontakis*
Roman Tsymbala
Mark-Anthony Turnage
Karen Tuttle
John Turturro

Aube Tzerko
Mitsuko Uchida
Shannon Unger
Alexandr Uninsky
Ayako Urushihara
Dawn Upshaw*
Wolfgang Vacano
William Vacchiano
Chris Vadala
Joaquin Valdepeñas*
Benita Valente
Fernando Valenti
Reza Vali
Irma Vallecillo*
Cesare Valletti
Monica Vanderveen
Gilbert Varga
Lászlo Varga
Milagro Vargas*
Paul Velucci
Martin Verdrager*
Ilana Vered*
Paul Vermel
Robert Vernon*
Shirley Verrett
Joe Vizzutti
Allan Vogel*
Arnold Voketaitis
Ealynn Voss
Franz Vote
Vitya Vronsky
Jan Wagner
Juergan Wahl
David Wakefield*
Linda Wall*
Richard Waller
Richard Walter
Lois Wann
Timothy Ward
Stanley Warren*
Marvin Warshaw*
Dionne Warwick
Akeo Watanabe
Howard Watkins
Bill Watrous
Ken Watson
André Watts*
Ernie Watts
Thomas Webb
David Weber
Beveridge Webster
Douglas Webster*
Virginia Weckstrom*
Alisa Weilerstein*
Donald Weilerstein*
Vivian Hornik

Weilerstein*
Frank Weinstock*
Lola Weir*
Dan Welcher*
Patricia Wells
August Wenzinger
Gary Werdesheim*
Michael Werner
Richard Wernick
Philip West
West End String Quartet
Richard Westenberg
Stig Westerberg
Fredrick Whang*
Kimball Wheeler*
Jiggs Whigham
Kathleen White*
John Reeves White
Robert White
Mark Whitfield
Bob Wilbur
David Wiley*
Jack Wilkins
Anne Martindale
    Williams
Camilla Williams

Joe Williams
Terry Tempest Williams
Erv Wilson
Harry Wimmer
Carol Wincenc*
David Winkler
Arthur Winograd
Peter Winograd*
William Winstead
Jessica Wolf
Duain Wolfe
Larry Wolfe
Hugh Wolff
Randall Wolfgang*
Richard Woodhams
Gary Woodward
Victor Lemonte Wooten
Margaret Jane Wray
Elizabeth Wright
Maurice Wright
Wu Han
Charles Wuorinen
Felix Wurman
Lisa Wurman
Susan Davenny Wyner*
Yehudi Wyner

Peter Wyrick*
Iannis Xenakis
Chen Xieyang*
Hiroko Yajima*
Won-Bin Yim
David Ying*
Ayako Yonetani*
Isang Yun
Anthony Zerbe
Tabea Zimmerman
David Zinman†
Brane Zivkovic
Frederick Zlotkin*
Linda Zoghby
Eugenia Zukerman*
Pinchas Zukerman
Paul Zukofsky*
Michele Zukovsky
Ellen Taaffe Zwilich

About the Author

BRUCE BERGER is the author of *The Telling Distance*, winner of the Western States Book Award and the Colorado Book Award, as well as *There Was A River, Almost an Island, The End of the Sherry*, his account of a lifetime in Aspen *The Complete Half-Aspenite*, and the poetry collection *Facing the Music*. While pursuing a B.A. in English at Yale University he studied piano at the Yale School of Music, has played professionally in the United States and Spain, and has given benefit concerts in Mexico. In 2008 he was sent by the Department of State to represent the United States at the Mussoorie International Writers' Festival in northern India, followed by a week of readings in New Delhi and Mumbai.